Jeremy Black is on⟨...⟩ ⟨...⟩o-
rians. He is Profess⟨...⟩ ⟨...⟩a
renowned expert on the history of war. His recent books include
A Brief History of Italy and *The World of James Bond*, which offers a
historian's perspective on the Bond novels and films. He appears
regularly on TV and radio, including BBC Radio 4's *In Our Time*.

A BRIEF HISTORY OF

PORTUGAL

....

JEREMY BLACK

ROBINSON

ROBINSON

First published in Great Britain in 2020 by Robinson

3 5 7 9 10 8 6 4 2

A CIP catalogue record for this book is available from the British Library.

ISBN: 978-1-47214-358-7

Typeset in Scala by Hewer Text UK Ltd, Edinburgh
Printed and bound in Great Britain by Clays Ltd, Elcograf S.p.A.

Papers used by Robinson are from well-managed forests and other responsible sources.

Robinson
An imprint of
Little, Brown Book Group
Carmelite House
50 Victoria Embankment
London EC4Y 0DZ

An Hachette UK Company
www.hachette.co.uk

www.littlebrown.co.uk

For Stephen Rathbone

Contents

Preface

One of the most interesting of Europe's countries, a nation of charming people, a landscape with historic cities and sandy beaches, Portugal has a long history of links with Britain and is visited by many British people. There are, indeed, some similarities between the geographies and cultures of the two countries. On the same time zone, they each were mighty empires, and, for most of the last six and a half centuries, their alliance has been significant to both.

However, despite the interest and importance of the Portuguese exploration of much of the world in the fifteenth and sixteenth centuries, including the maritime route to India, the Portuguese empire, and of such vivid episodes as the Lisbon Earthquake of 1755, Portugal's history, and that of Portugal's world, are generally unknown in Britain or, indeed, by most non-Portuguese people. Outside Portugal, its history is not widely taught or, usually, ever taught, at school or university level, or covered in film or television. I do not recall Portugal once being mentioned when I did history at school or, indeed, in the first two years of my course at Cambridge.

Whereas the history of Spain, Portugal's only neighbouring state, has attracted much international attention over the last forty years, and there has been a marked increase in Britain in learning Spanish and in Spanish food and culture, none has been true for Portugal. That is a mistake, for Portugal is a fascinating country and with an interesting history.

This book is designed to provide a succinct history aimed at the tourist. The intention is to be comprehensive, yet accessible. It will range across Portugal's history and geography. Allowing for this, the book will devote particular attention to three aspects: Portugal's global role, its historic links with Britain, and the history and character of Portugal's principal regions.

The global impact is clear. Indeed, as a result particularly of past rule in Brazil, Portuguese today is the sixth most widely spoken language in the world, after Chinese, Hindi, English, Spanish and Arabic. The global role first begins with the Portuguese age of exploration in the fifteenth century, notably with Prince Henry the Navigator and Vasco da Gama. This was not an age of discovery as the peoples reached knew they were there, while Europeans were already aware that India existed. But there was an exploration of new routes and the 'discovery' of peoples unknown to Europeans, notably those of Brazil. Portugal was the first of the Atlantic empires and also opened up the direct sea route from Europe to Asia, a route later to be followed by the Dutch and the English.

Fishing the Atlantic, the settlement of Madeira, the Azores and the Cape Verde Islands, and exploration of the west coast of Africa, were followed, from the mid-sixteenth century onwards, by a global empire that reached from Macao in China and Timor in the East Indies, via Malacca (Malaysia), Goa, other Indian positions, and bases in Sri Lanka, to Mombasa, Mozambique, other bases in East Africa, Angola, bases in West Africa, and then on to Brazil. Portugal had a major world empire until the loss of Brazil in the 1820s, Indian possessions until 1961, an African empire until 1975, and a surviving foothold in Asia until Macao was returned to China in 1999.

What remains territorially are only the Azores and Madeira. But what also remains, both in Portugal and more widely, is the legacy of a world empire, indeed of a particular type of world empire, a conflation of people, food, ideas, language, religion, culture, and an opening up to the outside that has left Portugal very different from much of southern Europe, including those other imperial powers, Spain and Italy.

As England's oldest ally, Portugal benefited from English help in the bloody tasks of conquering Lisbon from Moorish rule in 1147 and in opposing Castile in the fourteenth century. English longbowmen played a crucial part in the warfare of the 1380s, and notably in the battle of Aljubarrota in 1385. The English went on to play a key military role in Portuguese history in the 1580s, 1660s, 1700s, 1760s, 1808–13 and the 1820s: whereas in the 1580s Philip II of Spain was accepted by a substantial part of Portuguese society, from the 1660s English musketeers continued the early role of the archers in helping to secure Portugal's liberties.

Portugal remained an important ally for Britain, and the British wish that Portugal would accept this role was generally (but not always) reciprocated. Portugal was even an informal member of the British empire throughout the nineteenth century, albeit a forced one, as when George Canning remarked 'Portugal must always be English.' Indeed, the ultimatum in 1890 (see Chapter 10) was scarcely the product of an harmonious agreement over goals.

Trade was very important to Anglo-Portuguese relations, economic and political. This trade took English, later British, goods to Portugal, notably woollen cloth from the Middle Ages and coal in the nineteenth century. From Portugal and its empire came most famously port and gold, the former leaving a noted legacy in the repertoire of British drinks, the latter, from Brazil, important to the solvency of the British empire in the eighteenth century.

More recently, large-scale British tourism has developed, notably to the Algarve. Alongside the sun, beaches and golf there, Portugal for the British also means the major cruise stops in Lisbon, Oporto, Madeira and the Azores, the development of cruise holidays on the Douro, and city breaks to Lisbon and Oporto. Each of these have become popular. Moreover, it seems apparent that British tourism will remain important to the Portuguese.

Past Affection

On 13 May 1762, the *London Chronicle* reported:

> There is no state upon earth of which the Portuguese entertain so high an opinion as of ours, nor any people of whom they think or speak as well as of the English, whether in a collective sense as a nation, or an individual one as traders; while there are no nations, or people, which they equally hate with the French and Spaniards. So that, in spite of all their blind bigotry in religion (by which they are made to hate us as heretics) as a state, or as traders, their own interest and experience have attached them to us in the strongest manner.

National stereotypes are always dangerous if not misleading, and reading those of the past is to be struck by how much they date. Equally, it is worth noting the very frequent contrasting by British travellers of the Portuguese with the Spaniards, and always to the favour of the former who are generally presented as more relaxed and more friendly, the two being closely linked.

The history of Portugal's regions reflects in part their distinctive character, and also the interest of this very varied country. From the mountainous north to the cliffs and beaches of the Algarve in the south, from the mainland to the islands, Portugal is well worth visiting. The regions have the common history that is Portugal, but also different experiences, and their varied background provides tourists with a happy diversity within a relatively small space. Moreover, although some of the driving can be frightening and minor roads can be poor, it is easier to drive across Portugal than in the past.

Visiting Portugal on numerous occasions from 1990, I have always met with a friendly reception. This book is a small way of repaying that debt. I have benefited from the comments of Hélder Carvalhal, Roger Collins, Andrea Christina Naegele, Malyn Newitt and José Miguel Pereira Alcobio Palma Sardica on an earlier draft, and from the encouragement of Gabriel Paquette, Richard Stoneman, Peter Wiseman, Anthony Wright and Patrick Zutshi have provided advice on particular points. None is responsible for any errors that remain. Duncan Proudfoot has proved a most supportive editor.

It is a great pleasure to dedicate this book to Stephen Rathbone, a good friend of twenty-nine years standing and a sound guide to the issues of teaching well.

1. Introduction

The geography of Portugal explains its character. The interior is difficult to cultivate, with terrain and climate key problems, and repeatedly so. Yet Portugal also has a long coastline, indeed, for a part of a continental landmass, it has a high ratio of coastline to land area. If not as high as Denmark, the ratio is far higher than that for Spain. Moreover, while much of the country is close to the coast, an appreciable percentage is also close to rivers that flow there, and notably to the mighty Tagus, of which the extensive estuary provides the foreground for Lisbon. The major cities, Lisbon and Oporto, are ports and, across its over 500 miles of coastline, the country looks out to the Atlantic. Nearly half of the population lives in the Atlantic coastal strip from Braga, in the north, to Setúbal, south of Lisbon. Unlike for Spain, France and Britain, no other sea shares Portugal's attention.

For most of its history from the sixth century BCE (Before Common Era, or BC, Before Christ), the near-ocean offered fish, a plentiful source of protein and vitamins, albeit one that exposed fishermen to the threatening rollers and storms of the Atlantic, and to the hard work of working its waters. Fish quays and markets (as in Lisbon) offer much for tourists to see; the fish auctions at Cascais and Sesimbra, after the day's catch has been brought in, being of particular interest. The freshness of the fish can make nearby restaurants particularly appealing.

The broader horizon of the apparently limitless Atlantic, however, suggested limits, not opportunities, for a long time, indeed until the fifteenth century. Instead of being different, the population was affected by the broader currents of the history of the Iberian peninsula and had many similarities with that of Spain, with which it has an 800-mile border, a border that, since independence in the twelfth century, has always posed issues. For much of its history, Portugal had no obvious rationale, geographical or otherwise, for being treated as a separate entity. Indeed, its existence is purely the result of socio-political processes that date from no earlier than the ninth and tenth centuries, and that led, as a result of happenstance, to a separate political entity from the twelfth century. Thus, there is no distinct nor distinctive Portugal before the creation of that state.

Instead, like the rest of Iberia, Portugal experienced Roman conquest, Christianisation, Visigothic conquest, the Muslim takeover, the driving out of the Muslims, and the consolidation of a new kingdom. As in Spain, most of the population lived on the land and from agriculture. Both were part of the Iberian peninsula, Portugal constituting about one sixth of it. Portugal has no other borders.

Yet, the details of geography helped ensure that, although there was nothing to match the strength of regional identity and politics in Spain with its far more divided history and greater size, nevertheless there were important variations in the pattern of Portugal's character. These will be discussed in greater detail in Chapters 13 to 16, the regional part of the book, but, essentially, the mountainous, colder north contrasts with the drier south. However, as we will see, there are many other significant qualifications and variations. Each of these contributes to the fascination of Portugal and its ten million inhabitants.

A key element, however, across much of Portugal is the (varied) difficulty of the environment and, in particular, of the soil; although there are major exceptions including in Estremadura, notably near the Tagus. That harshness affects agricultural yields. Combined with the rocky terrain, this means that part of the country is not terribly suitable for farming, most clearly in the highest mountain range in mainland Portugal, the *Serra da Estrela*. However, this is not only a problem in high areas. Instead, repeatedly across Portugal, the rocks stick through the thin soil.

In addition, particularly in the north, the slopes can frequently be very steep. That contributes to the picturesque quality of the vineyards in the Douro Valley, but they are very difficult to work and certainly cannot be picked by machine. The profits from the sale of port ensure that handpicking is economic, although it also pushes up costs. Indeed, the difficulties posed by the steepness of the slopes across much of Portugal can be seen in the shape of abandoned farms, neglected terracing and deserted farmsteads. In contrast come the lush grassland plains near the Tagus, for example the Lezíria, an area noted for horse breeding and for the breeding of bulls for the popular sport of bullfighting.

An inherent inefficiency in some of the agriculture has been exposed, both since Portugal joined the EEC by a serious exposure to competition and because the challenge of mechanisation, which is not really so practical on stony soils, became more significant as agriculture elsewhere in Europe embraced machinery. As a result, there has been an abandonment of many fields that are on steep slopes, and especially of wheat production. Depopulation had been particularly acute in the rural areas of the north and the Beiras, and this continues to be the case. Portuguese dualism – the interior versus the coast – has been a long-standing structural feature of the country. Urbanisation in the 1950s and 1960s speeded up the process which has continued since.

Much else testifies to the challenges posed by the environment. Moreover, these can remain very difficult. Fire is a major hazard, and was notably so in June and October 2017, and July 2019. The heat of the summer and the readily inflammable nature of the woodland contribute to such cataclysms. Floods, in contrast, have become less of a problem. They used to be very serious, notably on the Douro before it was regulated by dams, but also on smaller rivers such as the Tâmega. The frequent flooding of the Mondego in Coimbra forced the closure of the Santa Clara convent in 1677 and its movement to a new site uphill. There were regular floods of the Tagus, notably near Santarém. The high-water marks in riverside towns, such as Amarante, are a clear legacy of floods, as are centres that were built safely above the riverbank, such as Régua on the Douro.

The Portuguese can make sardonic remarks about their climate, on the lines of nine months of winter and three months of hell. It can certainly be too hot to do much, and tourists, whether or not familiar with heat, are advised to pace themselves, especially, but not only, in the summer and notably so as they go further south. In the south, the buildings are often of clay, are whitewashed in order to help repel the sun, and have few openings, in order to keep the summer heat out. Moreover, there is frequent heavy rain in northern Portugal, both up to March (and sometimes until May) and after September. Without the rain, there would not be greenery and agriculture because most of the agriculture does not have the benefit of irrigation, which is less developed than in Spain.

In between, however, there is much good weather. April and May are the best months for travel, because the weather is good but the massive crowds that descend in the summer have not yet arrived. With recent trends, June is now one of the very busy months. As the crowds ease, September is also good; it can still have the summer heat while it is drier than the spring. The Algarve and Madeira attract many visitors in the winter, but not the Azores, which can be stormy as well as wet. For a Brit, the winter across central and northern Portugal may be wet, and a wet day in Oporto can be very wet and windy, but it is milder than in Britain. I have had a wonderful holiday in Lisbon and its environs in a December, with clear skies and weather that was both calm and warm enough to permit lunch outdoors.

All-year round, Portugal has much to offer. The conveniences of the present, from heaters to air-conditioning, spare the modern tourist many of the discomforts of his or her predecessors. So also with refrigeration for food preservation, the rapid distribution of food by road, road surfaces that permit smooth journeys, and the speed of modern vehicles. They shrink the country, but it still repays the detailed eye.

2. Prehistory and Classical Portugal: The Stone Age to the End of the Roman Era

Early Settlement

Portugal has a long history of human settlement. Early hominids lived there, and archaeological research over the last thirty years has provided fascinating evidence, even if the broader picture, as for other countries, can be elusive. *Homo antecessor*, the archaic *Homo sapiens*, were followed by Neanderthals and then by Cro-Magnon humans, the origins of modern *Homo sapiens*. There is evidence of the coexistence of Neanderthals and Cro-Magnon humans, and, in 1999, just north of Lisbon, a Palaeolithic skeleton with a legacy from both was discovered.

Initially cave-dwellers, the Cro-Magnon humans were able to range widely, using stone and composite tools, not least as weapons, and they developed skills accordingly. Cave drawings survive in the *Gruta do Escoural* in the Alentejo from around 15000 BCE and in the archaeological park of the Côa Valley. As in France and Spain, animals play an important role in these drawings. Early carvings can be seen in Oporto's *Soares dos Reis* museum. The *Grutas das Lapas*, caves near Torres Novas, were occupied in Neolithic times.

The ice ages provided major issues of adaptation as the climate cooled. Portugal was not covered in the i̶c̶e̶ ̶s̶h̶e̶e̶t̶ ̶t̶h̶a̶t̶ shrouded much of northern Europe. Nevertheless, i̶t̶ ̶w̶a̶s̶ ̶a̶f̶f̶e̶c̶t̶e̶d̶ by the major fall in temperature, by its savage effe̶c̶t̶s̶ ̶o̶n̶ ̶t̶h̶e̶ seasons, and by the falling of the sea level due to i̶c̶e̶ ̶a̶n̶d̶ water near the poles.

The subsequent rise in the temperature after the ice ages ended in about 10000 BCE saw far more benign environments for plants and, in part as a result, for animal life. Humans benefited, both as hunters and as gatherers, and the population rose. Larger mammals, however, could be badly affected by climate change and were also hunted to extinction. Evidence of hunter-gatherers has been found from around Alcácer even earlier, indeed back to the Mesolithic period about 40,000 years ago. The Sado Estuary was exploited including in searching for shellfish, a practice also seen in Japanese coastal waters.

In turn, cereal cultivation spread, with the domestication of wild crops and their propagation. There was also a domestication of animals that led to sheep and goat herding. As a consequence, the roaming and foraging lives of hunter-gatherers came to overlap and then be replaced by more sedentary lifestyles.

Thanks to the more intensive agriculture, villages that were probably inhabited year-long were established, for example on hilltops in the lower Tagus Valley in about 5000 BCE. Their setting provided protection. Such settlements saw the development of craft skills and trade, and had the manpower for building and for concerted activity.

Stone monuments, including megaliths round Évora and more generally in the Alentejo, are an important legacy. Particularly impressive is the *Cromeleque dos Almendres*, a far-flung oval of ninety-five granite monoliths ten miles west of Évora surrounded by a cork oak forest, and, nearby, the *Menir dos Almendres* and the *Anta Grande do Zambujeiro*, Europe's largest dolmen (single-chamber megalithic tomb). The remains from the last site are in Évora's museum. These megaliths indicate the sophistication of a society that used such sites for ritual practices and for astronomy. A considerable level of organisation is suggested by such works. There are also megalithic burial chambers in the region around Lisbon, although permanent settlements do not leave an haeological trace until about 2500 BCE.

The first known native people of Portugal date from the late Bronze Age (1100–700 BCE). Known as the *Estrímnios* (Latin: *Oestrimni*), they had fortified settlements in the valleys and on the estuaries of central Portugal. The archaeological record improves with the Iron Age, during which Celtic peoples, having crossed the Pyrenees, moved into Portugal in about 700 BCE, building fortified hill villages or *citânias*, such as *Sanfins de Ferreira* near Santo Tirso, a walled settlement with about a hundred huts. A key example is the *Citânia de Briteiros*, between Braga and Guimarães, which was inhabited from about 300 BCE. Protected by walls and supported by a water distribution system, it contained over 150 stone huts linked by paved paths. The site, which includes reconstructed huts, can be visited, while remains can be seen in Guimarães in the archaeological museum named after Martins Sarmento, who excavated the site, and also in his manor house. The former has Celtic sarcophagi and decorative stones from the Celtiberian bathhouses of the region. To the north-west, on the Mount of Santa Luzia near Viana do Castelo, the ruins of another *citânia* can be visited. Further south, Alcácer do Sal on the River Sado originated as an Iron Age hillfort. So also with Linhares and Monsanto.

The defensive character of such sites is readily apparent, not least in providing warnings of raiders. The sites served to protect people, their grain stores and their animals. So also with the defensive possibilities of Almourol, an island in the Tagus, where there was an Iron Age fort that was to be conquered and occupied by the Romans. Museums hold important material from the Iron Age. The regional archaeological museum in Chaves has bronze tools, grinding stones, which were crucial for milling grain, and jewellery. The museum of Dom Diogo de Sousa in Braga holds arrowheads, ceramics and funerary objects.

It is difficult to determine the relationship between the Celts and the pre-existing tribes. Alongside different cultural groups, there was probably much overlap, not least due to intermarriage;

but, in both cases, there are many difficulties involved in classification and in its application. Changes across time also entail questions about the causation of change.

Phoenicians and Greeks

The nature of the available archaeological and, later, written, records direct attention to external links and foreign intervention in Portugal. While important, these links and intervention can, however, lead to a serious underplaying of indigenous developments. The Iron Age saw the establishment of a Phoenician presence, with a nearby Phoenician mercantile base at *Gadir* (Cádiz) from about 800 BCE. Precious metals, especially copper, iron, tin, gold and silver, were their goal, and were well worth the journey. Tin was important for the production of bronze.

There were Phoenician colonies in Abul and Alcácer. Influence was not restricted to the coast. For example, the Rio Arade provided a river route into the Algarve, along which copper and iron could be transported for export. At Mértola on the River Guadiana, the Phoenicians had an inland trading position. Further north, there was another at Alcácer do Sal. Each were to be municipalities where the citizens had old Latin rights during the Roman Empire. In return for the precious metals the Phoenicians brought Mediterranean goods, such as wine and textiles. Trade, moreover, became the means for technological and cultural transmission. In the eighth century BCE, the Phoenicians established a position in Lisbon which they called *Alis Ubbo* or calm harbour. The site was on the southern slope of the castle hill.

There may also have been a Greek trading station there, and the Greeks appear to have established a presence in Portugal in the sixth century BCE. Their trade was similar to that of the Phoenicians. Indeed, the Latin name for Lisbon, *Olisipo*, was said in Late Antique and Phoenician tradition to derive from the fact that Ulysses (*Ulixes*) went there in his wanderings.

Phoenician influences came to be directed by Carthage, a dynamic Phoenician settlement near modern Tunis. It became a major power and established a significant presence in southern and eastern Spain, but not in distant Portugal, although the latter was probably within the ambit of Carthaginian commercial influence. Carthaginian attempts at conquest were allegedly unsuccessful.

Roman Conquest

Having conquered the Carthaginian bases and territories in Spain during the Second Punic War (218–201 BCE), Carthage's nemesis, Rome, eventually sought to extend its power across the entire peninsula. From the Guadalquivir Valley in nearby Andalusia from 208 BCE, the Romans began to press on nearby southern Portugal. Yet, the Romans found that there was a major difference between overthrowing another foreign imperial presence, in the shape of Carthage, and subjugating the rest of Iberia. The former was more vulnerable to attack, and more focused on cities, notably ports, that could be besieged. The targets in the remainder of Iberia were far more diffuse. This helps explain the length of time it took for the Romans to conquer Portugal, but there were more significant issues, notably the culture of conquest and, separately, alternative commitments. The Republican system with its annual consulates and praetorships functioned to give the officeholders brief opportunities for military glory, ideally winning triumphs as well as the profits to be made from war including slaves. So it was in the interests of the ruling elite in Rome to win victories and take loot but, at the same time, keep the war going almost indefinitely. The same situation occurred later in the early Islamic period. The Umayyads could in practice have eliminated the small Christian states in the north in the eighth, ninth and tenth centuries, but needed them as targets for annual campaigning, to advertise their credentials as Islamic rulers.

Returning to the long time the Roman conquest took, Rome, having defeated Carthage, was drawn into a series of wars with Macedon that left it in control of Greece, but that had absorbed much of Rome's energy through to 148 BCE. There were also other major struggles, including war further east with the Seleucid king, Antiochus, in 192–189 BCE, as well as the Third Punic War with Carthage (149–146 BCE).

Nevertheless, Rome made gains in this period in Iberia, and these gains were followed in 139–133 BCE by the successful conquest of much of Iberia. The *Lusitani*, a tribal confederation, probably Celtic, between the Tagus and the Douro, had provided firm resistance from 194 BCE, notably in 147–139 BCE under Viriathus, but his death was followed by Roman conquest. The Roman account was that Viriathus was killed in his sleep by his companions who had been bribed by the Romans, only for them to receive execution as their reward on the grounds that Rome did not pay traitors.

The Roman conquest involved local support, a practice also seen elsewhere. The city of *Olisipo* (Lisbon) provided help against the *Lusitani* from 138 BCE, and the Romans fortified the settlement. In 137 BCE, Roman forces, moving north, crossed the Douro and, the following year, reached the River Minho. The Roman troops proved reluctant to cross the rivers, fearing that they were the Lethe, the river of forgetfulness.

Julius Caesar, Governor of Hispania Ulterior, and after whom Beja was named *Pax Julia*, campaigned in what is now modern Portugal, north of the Tagus, conquering local tribes in 61–60 BCE. Aside from conquering, the Romans also faced rebellions, both from the indigenous population and, as elsewhere in the empire, from Roman rebels. With reference to Caesar's campaigns against Pompey's sons in Iberia in 45 BCE, a Roman writer noted: 'in view of the constant sallies of the natives, all places which are remote from towns are firmly held by towers and fortifications . . . they have watch-towers in them.'

Resistance to Roman conquest continued in north-west Spain and northern Portugal until 17 BCE, and this impressed Roman commentators, as well as providing a way to praise their own successes. In the nineteenth century, this resistance attracted interest from nationalist commentators and artists engaged with the idea of an exemplary pre-Roman national origin and concerned to trace difference from Spain to pre-Roman tribes. However, there was a marked preference, instead, for claiming a Roman legacy and for focusing, not on the resistance to the Romans, but, instead, on the eventually successful medieval resistance to the Muslims. The latter resistance could be presented as having an exemplary Christian character. Alongside the strength of the resistance came the many challenges to the Roman troops posed by the environment, notably those of operating in the mountains, of the climate and of logistical support.

Roman Rule

By the time the conquest of Iberia was complete, most of what would become Portugal was already part of the Roman system. Iberia was significant as a source of food and minerals, for example of gold from near Oporto. Establishing large agricultural estates (*latifúndios*), the Roman developed viticulture and the cultivation of grain and olives. Wool and horses were other significant exports to Italy, as well as elsewhere in the empire. Such estates were presumably linked to villas, a good example of which is the first century CE *Vila Cardílio* near Torres Novas. The baths survive, as do mosaics.

Roads were built by the Romans, originally in order to exert power and authority, notably to move troops for conquest and counter-insurgency. Near Porto de Mós, there is a Roman road that has become a walking trail. The roads constituted a system. Road junctions, such as *Bracara Augusta* (Braga), became significant settlements which, in turn, were crucial to the economy and, in particular, to the movement of goods. From Braga, roads ran to *Olisipo*, the sole municipality of Roman citizens in modern Lisbon in Pliny's time, and to Astorga in Spain. The associated bridges, which were important to the system, could be impressive. The Roman bridge at Ponte de Lima, en route from Braga to Astorga, mostly dates from the fourteenth century, but a segment of the Roman original survives. Finished in 104 CE, the 140-metre-long Roman bridge at Chaves survives with its arches and two milestones.

Not being on the Mediterranean, Roman Portugal was less well-integrated into the empire than much of Spain. Lusitania, the province covering much of what would become Portugal and western Castile, had its capital at *Emerita Augusta*, Mérida in modern Spain, and the scale of the theatre, amphitheatre and temple of Diana there in part reflect the tax revenues raised in Portugal.

Yet, thanks to the ports, for example modern Oporto, Lisbon, Alcácer and Alvor, goods could be exported directly from Portugal, such as salt from Vila do Conde. Moreover, there were also significant Roman building works in Portugal, notably at *Conímbriga* near Coimbra. Originally a Celtic settlement, this became a city on the route from Lisbon to Braga. Tourists can visit the remains of baths and luxurious villas, which have attractive mosaic floors, notably the extensive *Casa das Fontes* (House of Fountains). In Lisbon, where the population under the Romans may have been around 30,000, recent building work in the BCP bank has revealed the remains of a Roman fish-preserving plant which can be seen in the *Núcleo Arqueológico*. Fish-sauce (*garum*) was important to Roman cuisine and helped bring wealth to the city. Fish-salting was also carried out in *Cetóbriga*, a town near Troía where the stone tanks can be visited. Also in Lisbon are the remains of a Roman theatre, dating from 57 CE, and an accompanying museum which provides relevant information. Most of Roman Lisbon, however, has been destroyed and built over to a degree that there is nothing left.

Buildings focused on the cities: the forcing houses of Romanisation; the centres of government and of Roman religious cults; and the locations to which the wealth generated in the countryside was transferred, notably through taxes, rent and expenditure. Landowners tended to live in the cities, where Roman dress and the Latin language were adopted. Thus, *Conímbriga* had a forum and a bathing complex, while, in Évora, it is possible to visit the remains of the Roman baths, only discovered from 1987, as well as of a temple, generally referred to as a temple of Diana. In Braga, there are numerous remains, including the ruins of a theatre and baths that date from the second century CE, as well as the first-century Fountain of the Idol, which was associated with a water cult dedicated to a local Lusitanian god, *Tongoenbiagus*. The *Casa do Infante* in Oporto has Roman foundations and mosaics on show.

Most modern cities trace their origins to the Roman period or to the Roman development of Celtic sites. Thus, Leiria was the Roman *Collipo*, while Faro was *Ossonoba* and its archaeological museum contains a very impressive Roman mosaic. Many, such as Santarém (Roman *Scalabis*) were the administrative capitals of a region. However, some Roman cities did not have this legacy. *Egitânia* is the site today of only a small village, Idanha-a-Velha, although the cathedral holds a large collection of Roman epigraphs. Roman remains can also be found in the shape of country villas, such as that at Pisões near Beja, where the mosaics and baths can be visited.

As elsewhere in the empire, Romanisation was much weaker in areas that were mountainous and/or remote from cities, and where the economy was more a matter of subsistence and/or pastoral agriculture. That description covered most of Portugal. Moreover, this distinction remained pertinent across Portugal's history. There are, however, remains in these areas. For example, the *Centum Cellas*, a Roman tower, survives in Beira Baixa, although its function is unclear.

Portugal was affected by the more general developments of the Roman Empire, ranging from politics to the spread of disease. Knowledge about Portugal spread. Thus, it is covered in the *Geographica* of the Greek geographer Strabo (*c.* 63 BCE–24 CE), who was born in modern-day Turkey and wrote about the known world. Strabo referred to the wealth of Iberia as having attracted conquerors, and to Iberia as temperate thanks to its oceanic climate. He noted the production of copper, gold, salt and cloth, the poverty of much of the soil, and that northern Iberia was cold and rugged. Pliny, in his *Natural History*, wrote that from the Pyrenees to the Douro, the entire region was 'full of mines of gold, silver, iron, lead and tin'. He reported that gold was found in the River Tagus in the form of auriferous sands, and that Lisbon was 'famous for its mares which conceive from the west wind'. Pomponius Mela, who was writing in about 43–4 CE and came from near Gibraltar, referred to gems in the Tagus.

Developments subsequently included the diffusion of new religions, such as Mithras. Judaism, an old religion, spread as a consequence of the Jewish diaspora that followed the suppression of the revolt in Palestine in 132 CE. Judaism was also diffused in the new and very different form of Christianity, which was able to spread without ethnic limits. In 312, Christianity became the official religion of the empire. It was rapidly established and left a major imprint in the cities of the later empire where churches were built. Alcácer (*Salatia*) had a bishop in about 300 and Braga certainly had a bishop in around 390. The *Núcleo Arqueológico* in Lisbon includes the remains of a fifth-century Christian burial place. Although born in Rome, Pope Damasus I (r. 366–84) had parents who originated in Lusitania, possibly in *Egitânia*.

The cities of what became Portugal were heavily fortified in response to attacks from 'barbarians', which became serious in the 260s. In *Conímbriga*, a large wall was erected through the town centre. There was also political, fiscal and economic instability within the empire itself, and Portugal briefly became part of a rebel Roman Empire based in Gaul (France) under Postumus. Aurelian (r. 270–5) reunited the Roman Empire, however, and brought a measure of revival.

To strengthen the administration, Diocletian (r. 284–305) redrew provincial boundaries and introduced a system of joint rule that saw Iberia linked with Italy and North Africa. This, however, did not provide lasting stability and, instead, looked toward the lasting division of the Eastern and Western Empires in 395. Iberia was part of the more vulnerable, and less well-resourced West, and was invaded in 409 by Germanic tribes, the 'barbarians' that had emerged in Scandinavia during the Nordic Bronze Age of 1700–500 BCE before moving south, eventually forming migrating tribal entities.

Roman influence in Portugal continued, but it had been fatally weakened and, as with England, political and military links with Rome were sundered in the 410s. Lisbon was ravaged by the Visigoths in 419, and was captured by the Suevi in 469. They had destroyed once-impressive *Conímbriga* the previous year.

The Legacy of Rome

Although this legacy was much shadowed by 'barbarian' conquest and its later consequences, Roman rule left Latinity, Christianity, an urban structure and an experience of unity, as well as remains that are not only still impressive but also helped define the imagination of Rome's successors. Archaeology has helped expand our knowledge of Roman Portugal, and has provided more sites for tourists, as well as more material to consider in museums. There is still more to excavate, including at *Conímbriga*.

Although the legacy of Roman rule was significant, it was, and is, far less present than in Italy or, indeed, Spain. Instead, like Britain, what became Portugal absorbed the Roman legacy, and used it to justify its colonial rule, but rather shrugged off the administrative legacy of Roman rule, focusing instead on the long centuries of state formation in the medieval period.

In the case of Portugal, this process was accentuated because it was only then, and indeed over seven hundred years after Roman rule ceased, that Portugal became a separate state. In contrast, the Roman period was very much one of subordination within an Iberia in which Spain was clearly dominant. Moreover, Roman Portugal did not produce emperors, as Spain did with Trajan and Hadrian.

Later Portuguese writers did not devote much attention to the period of Roman rule or to the enduring legacy of Rome. So also with other aspects of Portuguese culture and, today, with representations of Portuguese history. Even Christianity, a key development of the Roman period, was removed from that mooring. In large part, this was because the emphasis, instead, was on Portuguese Christianity as the product of the driving back of the Moors. Thus, the post-Roman period of Suevi and Visigoth rule was also underplayed. Another approach would be to argue that the origins of Portugal really are twelfth century and were centrally focused on this driving back of the Moors.

Other countries have looked back to distant origins, most prominently Greece, and have underplayed, in contrast, the shorter process that deserves attention. This has not been the Portuguese course. Indeed, the theme of Roman rule was not really welcome because it focused attention not only on foreign control, but also on the issue of Spanish rule or rule as part of a Spanish-dominated Iberia as, under the Romans, that was the pattern of administration on the peninsula.

3. Suevi, Visigoths and Moors

The Suevi

Initially, western Iberia was overrun by the invading Suevi, a 'barbarian' people who swore fealty to the Western Emperor Honorius and created a sub-Roman kingdom from 410 to 585. The extent of their territories was restricted in the 450s by the expansionist Visigoths, another 'barbarian' people, with the Suevi driven into northern Portugal and Galicia. This was an aspect of the more general jostling between peoples, a process also seen in Italy, France, England and Scotland, that is obscure but that was important to what would later be seen as state and nation building. Later writers keen on tracing the separation of Portugal from Spain emphasised contrasts between the Suevi and the Visigoths. The extent of such contrasts, however, is problematic.

Braga became the Suevi capital. Church synods were held in Braga in 563, 572 and 675 in order to regularise conduct. Twelve bishops assisted in that held in 572. Braga had been elevated to the dignity of a metropolitan see in the mid-fifth century. Relatively little, however, is known about the Suevi.

The Visigoths

Affected by division, the Suevi were converted to Catholic Christianity in the sixth century, with several accounts being offered of this process. They finally merged with both the Visigoths and the local population in the late sixth century, with the last king deposed by his Visigoth rival, Leovigild, in

585, when Suevic or Suebic Galicia became the sixth province of the Visigothic kingdom. With the Visigoths in control of all of Iberia, bar the Balearic Islands, from 624, Portugal was thus again part of a larger state, albeit not now one ruled from Italy. The Visigoths continued Roman administrative structures and Latin, and renounced the Arian heresy in favour of Catholicism.

The Visigothic period has left a legacy of churches, and of gold and silver jewellery, although 'Visigothic' when applied to architecture, etc. is merely a chronological marker and not an ethnic one. It is just the date that makes these churches, arches and so on Visigothic. Moreover, the term Visigothic was not used in this period. Instead, the identity that was being forged was Gothic: *gens et patria Gothorum.*

Allowing for this, there are Visigothic remains in a number of museums including that in Coimbra. At Balsemão near the Douro, there is a Visigothic chapel probably dating from the sixth century. It is transitional, with Corinthian columns and round arches. Based on the church, the columns of which are Visigothic, Beja has a Visigothic museum. In nearby Mértola, there is a Visigothic area and an early Christian church. Subsequently created or reworked by medieval invention, the Visigothic period also left saints, for example the purely legendary Santa Iria (*c.* 635–*c.* 653), a nun allegedly murdered as a result of her chastity who became the patron saint of her birthplace, Tomar, and after whom the name of the town of *Scalabis* was changed to Santarém.

However, the churches were to be seized by Moorish invaders and destroyed or transformed. Thus, the Romanesque cathedral that was begun in Idanha-a-Velha in about 585 was transformed into a mosque. The Visigothic legacy is largely a matter of the archaeological record and that is limited because of the relative poverty of the period, and certainly limited compared to those of the Romans and the Moors, both of whom, of course, were also in control for far longer. Aside from poverty, revenues, in state and church, were moved eastward to the centres of Visigothic power, notably Toledo.

Moorish Conquest

The rapid fall of Iberia to Moorish invaders in, and after, 711 was one of the many dramatic successes by the forces of Islam. Explanations in Christian Iberia of its fall were for long religious, providential and moral: 'God testing His People' as well as the 'Coming of Antichrist' were key themes. There was also a theme of judgement in a story of rape, revenge and betrayal, in which a rape by Roderic, the last king, played a central role. In practice, Visigothic failure was due to Muslim strengths as well as Visigothic disadvantages, notably divisions and other military commitments including that against the recalcitrant Basques.

Crossing the Strait of Gibraltar in 711, as part of a much wider process of Islamic expansion that also soon after took Islamic forces up against the Chinese, the Moors defeated and killed Roderic that year or the next, following up by rapidly taking over most of Iberia. The Moors pressed on to invade France, where, in contrast to north-western Iberia, the south provided readily accessible targets. Initially successful, they were, however, heavily defeated at Tours in 732 or 733, with the crucial loss of leaders, and were driven out of France, losing the major city of Narbonne in 759.

Meanwhile, the Cantabrian Mountains had helped make the north, more particularly the north-west, of Iberia difficult for Muslim attackers to access, and had thereby provided refuge for the Christians. This refuge served as the foundation for a medieval Christian Portugal and Spain that were defined by war with the Moors and both based for long in the north. At the same time, the inhospitable lands of the north were of only limited interest to the Moors.

In contrast, having been exploited for taxation and labour, much of the Christian population in the Muslim areas eventually adopted Muslim culture and language. The extent of early Islamicisation is a matter of controversy, however, and there were relatively few places to worship Islam. The process of Islamicisation appears to have escalated in the tenth century.

Moorish Rule

Islamic Spain was ruled by the Umayyad caliphate of Córdoba and its wealth was focused in the south, notably in the valley of the Guadalquivir. Córdoba had its heyday in the mid-tenth century, under Abd-ar-Rahman III (r. 912–61) and his impressive successor as caliph, Al-Hakam II (r. 961–76). In the mid-tenth century, the advancing Christians were pushed back to the Douro, Coimbra being recaptured in 955.

In what was to become Portugal, a series of settlements meanwhile developed under Islamic rule, notably the towns of Lisbon (*Al-Ushbuna*) and Silves. At *Al-Ushbuna*, there was a palace on the site of the present castle, while the place name *Alfama* for part of Lisbon is a corruption of the Moorish *alharma* or hot springs. The geographer Idrisi described Silves, on the Rio Arade in the Algarve, then known as Shelb or Xelb, as attractive, wealthy and populous. Revealed by archaeology, Muslim remains can be found there, notably with the vaulted cistern in the castle, the well and wall section in the archaeological museum, and the mosque under the cathedral. However, Silves was sacked by the Christians in 1189. Moorish cisterns and wells can be found in a number of places, including the Moorish castle in Sintra.

More generally, Muslim crops, methods and words were brought in, including the cultivation of rice, saffron and citrus fruit, words such as *arroz* (rice), the use of water mills, and place names, including the Algarve. In the last, the chimneys reflect Moorish influence in their style and decoration. The half-cylindrical roof tiles and glazed tiles found across Portugal originated with the Moors. Although the Moors reached far to the north, they settled particularly in the Algarve, the Tagus Valley and the Alentejo. The milder climate of the south attracted them, as did the extent to which this was already a well-worked landscape, with agricultural estates and towns. In contrast, there was scant Moorish settlement north of Coimbra and, even more, north of the Douro.

The emirate of Córdoba was under pressure from the expanding Christian kingdoms of northern Iberia, which, in the case of what became Portugal, was that of León. However, more significantly, division within Córdoba, notably between the Berbers and others groups, was triggered by rivalry over the position of caliph, with civil war breaking out in 1009. This led to the fragmentation of the caliphate into a number of independent kingdoms or *ta'ifas*. The most important of these was based on Seville, which gradually became pre-eminent in southern Spain, and included the Algarve. To its north-west, the kingdom of Badajoz, also with its capital in modern Spain, included Lisbon and what is now central Portugal. This fragmentation provided opportunities for the Christian kingdoms to press the *Reconquista* forward.

Under pressure from the Christians, some of the Muslims, in 1086, disenchanted with *ta'ifa* rule, called in the Almoravids, recently converted Saharan Berbers, who, taking advantage of the vacuum left by the collapse of Umayyad power, had overrun Morocco in the 1060s. They took over most of the *ta'ifas*, Badajoz falling to them in 1094. However, some of Muslim Spain resisted the Almoravid takeover in the 1090s, and this situation contributed greatly to the extent to which there could be cooperation between Christian and Moors.

In 1139, Afonso Henriques, the grandson of Alfonso VI of León, supposedly with the help of St James, won a major victory at Ourique. Thanks to this victory and, more generally, the process discussed in the following chapter, the county of Portucale became a kingdom, with the capital at Coimbra from 1143, and not, as had been declared by Afonso in 1128, Guimarães further north. Under growing pressure across Iberia from the Christians, the Almoravids, also affected by dynastic disunity, were overthrown from the 1150s by the Almohads, Shi'ite Berber sectarians who had already conquered Morocco in the 1140s. The Almohads went on to conquer the rest of Muslim Spain. They lent new energy to Muslim resistance.

The different periods of Muslim rule were characterised by contrasting emphases in architecture and the decorative arts. Thus, Almohad architecture had a simpler style than that of the earlier Córdoban caliphate.

In the thirteenth century, the Muslims were driven back. Their defeat was linked to the collapse of the Almohad Empire as a result of succession disputes after the defeat of Yusuf II in 1224. As Almohad forces were transferred to Morocco in order to fight a Marinid insurgency, Muslim Iberia was divided, and the Christians were able to find local allies. The Almoravids, Almohads and Marinids successively show how the history of Portugal was greatly affected by developments in North Africa because these destabilised Muslim Iberia. This linkage helps explain subsequent Portuguese interest in the fate of Morocco. In 1242, the town of Tavira close to the Algarve coast was captured by Dom Paio Peres Correia. Faro followed seven years later. This decade was the end of Moorish Portugal.

The Moorish Legacy

As with earlier periods of Portuguese history, that under the Moors did not have a lasting resonance in terms of Portugal's image of its past. There is a marked contrast with modern Spain, not least with the lack of any significant current focus on past cooperation between Moors, Christians and Jews, a focus that has attracted attention in Spain in terms of *al-Andalus*. Nor are there any comparisons in Portugal with the scale and beauty of the sites of Moorish Spain, notably Granada and Córdoba, nor with the literature and art later devoted to them by Western writers and artists. Moreover, Moorish Spain lasted until 1492, a quarter-millennium longer than Moorish Portugal, with a major rebellion occurring thereafter in 1568–70; and thus the Moors had a longer resonance in Spanish history than is the case for Portugal.

These points help address the question of whether there is a misleading amnesia as far as Portugal's Moorish past is concerned. This is a less than fair criticism given the extent to which there has not really been an obvious impact to the present. Nor is there a large Islamic minority today that needs to be addressed in terms of an historical account, or close political or cultural relations with North-west Africa. Tourists can construct an itinerary focusing on Moorish sites in Portugal, but they are relatively few, and tourists with these interests would be far better advised to turn to southern Spain. In part, that is also a reflection of the extent to which Moorish Portugal was peripheral not only to the Moorish world as a whole, but also to the Moorish empires based in southern Spain and/or spanning Iberia and Morocco. This marginality understandably directs attention to the independent Christian state that emerged from overturning Moorish Portugal, and with scant continuity between them.

4. Medieval Portugal

Under Moorish Pressure

The Cantabrian Mountains of northern Spain had provided refuge for the Christians. This refuge served as the basis for a medieval Christian Iberia defined by war with the Muslims. Rejecting the latter culturally, as well as in political and religious terms, the Christians sought to assert continuity with the Visigoths and, through them, with the Romans. Thus, Bishop Pelayo of Oviedo (r. 1098/1101–1130) claimed that the relics of major saints were brought north from the Visigoth capital, Toledo, in the time of the kingdom of the Asturias (c. 718–910). His claims, however, were untrue and were aspects of the truth by fabrication that was important to the assertion of continuity. Separately, the invocation of Visigothic law remained a standard procedure in courts in northern Iberia. The Christian north was also an area in which monasteries were established. Artistic motifs developed, and these were linked to patterns elsewhere in Christendom. Thus, Romanesque-style horseshoe arches featured in churches built from the ninth century.

Religious conviction then has left a range of stories and cults to the present. At Nazaré, it is possible in the Baroque church of Our Lady of Nazareth to see a sculpture of the Virgin that was allegedly made by Joseph. It is also possible there to see paintings that refer to a local legend, that of how the Virgin in 1182 saved a local noble from following the deer he was chasing into a chasm. At the site, a chapel was built to give thanks and to house a statue of the Virgin. Further south, at Cabo Espichel, a thirteenth-century vision of the Madonna coming out of the sea on a mule led to the site becoming a pilgrimage destination that has lasted as such to the present.

Frequent warfare, however, brought devastation to the north until the Muslims were pushed south. There was also incessant conflict within, and between, the small Christian principalities, as authority was asserted and power contested. This incessant situation was encouraged by the extent to which the legitimation of authority rested on power, and doubly so due to the lack of any true cohesion in what was a warband society adopting feudalism. Moreover, notions of legitimation were affected by the difficulty of fixing succession practices, let alone rules, a situation seen more widely in medieval Christendom, that lasted for Portugal into the early nineteenth century.

However, the focus in conflict was that between these principalities and the Muslims. Muslim raiding was for long a major aspect of life in the principalities. It had functional purposes in the quest for booty, notably slaves. There were also, certainly later, ideological goals, particularly the punishment of unbelievers. The determination of men to assert their role and masculinity through military activity was very important.

The Drive Southwards

There was counter-raiding by the Christian principalities, including of Lisbon in 798, as well as territorial expansion southward and political ambition. Asturias expanded southward in the ninth century and became the kingdom of León. Vímara Peres, a vassal of the ruler, was named count of Portugal in 868 after he conquered the region north of the Douro, including Oporto. He founded a fortified town, Vimaranis, which became present day Guimarães. A modern statue of him is by the cathedral in Oporto, and one of the major streets there is named after him. The second count of Portugal within the kingdom was his son, Lucídio Vimaranes, jointly with Hermenegildo Gutiérrez. These two families dominated the governorship of the county until the eleventh century. This is an obscure period and, to follow it, it is necessary to note references to individuals in charters. Portugal comes from Portucale, which is based on the Roman settlements of Portus and Cale on the Douro estuary. Portus became Oporto.

In the tenth century, Córdoba resumed incursions into northern Iberia, recapturing Coimbra. However, in the eleventh century, after civil war broke out in Córdoba in 1009, the Christian states began to take advantage of what was happening, and increasingly took the initiative. Oporto had already been reconquered by 1000, followed by Braga in 1040 and Lamego in 1057. In 1064, Ferdinand I of Castile and León captured Coimbra.

The last count of Portugal from the family of Vímara Peres, Nuno Mendes, sought greater autonomy, which led to his being defeated and killed at the battle of Pedroso in 1071. The victor, King García II of Galicia, a son and heir of Ferdinand I and Sancha of León, whose Leónese inheritance included the lands García would be given, then called himself king of Galicia and Portugal. He was the first to call himself king of Portugal. García, who had succeeded to his estates in 1065, had territory south to the River Mondego, as well as tribute from the Arab rulers of Badajoz and Seville. His reign saw the re-establishment of bishoprics, including at Braga and Lamego, as a way to assert royal authority and to demonstrate legitimacy.

In 1071, however, García was attacked by his brother Alfonso VI of León (r. 1065–1109), who invaded Portugal, only for the latter to be defeated in 1072 by their other brother, Sancho II of Castile (r. 1065–72), with whom he had jointly dispossessed García the previous year. Sancho, who was helped by El Cid (which means 'The Lord'), was crowned king of León, but was assassinated with the use of his own sword later that year. Alfonso regained his throne, reuniting Ferdinand I's kingdom, helped by his imprisoning García for the rest of the latter's life. Galicia was to stay with León and Castile, and not be part of Portugal as might otherwise have appeared logical.

Many castles remain from the eleventh century, including the domineering one at Penela and also that at Arouca. Much of central Portugal was overrun by the Christians at the end of the century but the Almoravid victory at Sagrajas, north of Badajoz, in 1086 was a major blow that stopped the advance. So also with the battle of Uclés in 1108. In contrast to the emphasis on heavy cavalry in conflict in France, in Portugal, as in Spain, there was a far greater stress on light cavalry. This proved more effective against the Moors, less expensive, and better attuned to the hot and arid environment.

Alfonso VI was succeeded by his eldest child, Urraca, who was married to Raymond of Burgundy. Their son was Alfonso VII (r. 1126–57), under whom León proved particularly strong. Crowned Emperor of Spain (like his grandfather and mother), Alfonso VII, who inherited the united throne of León, Castile and Galicia, campaigned against the Almoravids, and expanded his power southward to the Tagus, in turn raiding well south of there.

Alfonso VII divided his kingdom between his sons, so Castile separated from León in 1157. Portugal had already become fully independent in 1143 under Afonso Henriques (Afonso I), victor over the Muslims at Ourique in 1139. He was a son of Henry of Burgundy, himself a grandson of Duke Robert I of Burgundy, who had arrived the previous century in order to pursue his fortune and had married Teresa (illegitimate daughter of Alfonso VI), and therefore a grandson of Alfonso VI. Henry was a brother of Raymond of Burgundy. In 1086, Alfonso VI had appealed for help against the Almoravids, which led to the Burgundians going to Portugal. Henry had been made count of Portugal by Alfonso in 1096. Teresa became count of Portugal in 1112 on the death of her husband during the siege of Astorga.

Becoming Independent

In 1127, Afonso Henriques revolted against Teresa. He defeated his mother in 1128 at the battle of São Mamede near Guimarães, establishing his control of Portugal, over which he proclaimed himself prince in 1129. He then turned on the Moors, capturing Leiria in 1135 and winning a major victory at Ourique in 1139. At Lamego in 1143, Afonso convened a *cortes* (parliament) that confirmed him as King Afonso I. Victory at Valdevez in 1140 or 1141 had led to the Treaty of Zamora (1143) by which unwilling León, under his cousin Alfonso VII, recognised Portugal as sovereign. In 1179, the title was confirmed by Pope Alexander III, after the earlier pope, Lucius II, had refused recognition because he did not want Iberia divided but rather united against the Moors. The recognition of kingship was important not only insofar as independence from the Spanish rulers was concerned but also was related to the process by which political authority was increasingly considered as hereditary property. This was linked to a longer term consolidation of territory under fewer sovereigns and patriarchal dynasties.

War was a key theme, one reflected in surviving buildings such as Leiria castle. The Romanesque cathedral at Coimbra, built by Afonso I for a bishopric created in 1064, could also serve as a fortress with its crenellations and narrow windows. In 1147, Afonso pressed south in what became a key campaign for the history of Portugal. Lisbon, Santarém and Sintra were captured from the Moors, Porto de Mós following in 1148. English crusaders, en route to the Holy Land, played a major role in the bloody siege of Lisbon. By the time of Afonso's death in 1185, the frontier was well to the south, Beja falling in 1162, Évora in 1165 and Olivenza in 1170. Évora became a bishopric in 1166.

There are many memorials to this process. Évora has a statue of Gerald the Fearless, Portugal's El Cid, decapitating a Moor, and has him on its coats of arms, while its central plaza, the

Praça do Geraldo, is named after him. He also conquered Trujillo and Cávares. However, Portuguese expansion led to rivalry with Ferdinand II of León, and this produced conflict in 1169, with Ferdinand capturing some of Portugal's recent gains. Gerald pressed on to capture Beja in 1172, before falling out with Afonso I and, like another El Cid, putting himself in the service of the caliph.

Ecclesiastical independence from Spain had already been established. Part of northern Portugal had been under the archdiocese of Santiago de Compostela, where relics of Saint James made the see more potent. Toledo, the ancient Visigothic primatial see, reconquered in 1085, was the other source of ecclesiastical authority, but, in 1110, Braga was restored to its former role as an archbishopric, and was thus not under Toledo, with which relations had long been poor. This was a key element in what became Portuguese separation from Spain, and one of lasting significance due to the importance of clerics in culture and society. In 1390, the province of Braga was divided to create the archdiocese of Lisbon. By then the largest city in the kingdom, it had been made capital by Afonso III in 1256, replacing Coimbra, and its status had increased in 1173 when the relics of St Vincent were transferred from the Algarve. Relics were a crucial form of legitimation. Henry of Burgundy had made the Moorish citadel in Lisbon a royal palace. The central role of the Crown in driving back the Moors helped ensure that the Church in Portugal was very much under royal control.

There was a measure of Muslim push-back under the Almohads, including the defeat of Afonso I at Badajoz in 1170 and the recapture of Olivenza in 1189, but their siege of Santarém failed in 1184. Afonso was succeeded by his son, Sancho I (r. 1185–1211). Focusing on expansion to the south, he captured and fortified Silves in 1189, only to lose it in 1191 when he had to turn north to respond to the revived threat from León and Castile, which led him to found Guarda in 1197 and to reconstruct and repopulate Monsanto. Sancho was also noted for his attempts to populate remote parts of northern Portugal.

Sancho's successor, Afonso II (r. 1211–23), did not concentrate on expansion against the Moors and, instead, focused on developing the existing state, not only by introducing written laws but also by trying to limit the dominant position of the Church. This led to his being excommunicated by Pope Honorius III. However, the crushing victory, in a crusade, of Alfonso VIII of Castile, with support from Aragón, Navarre and Portugal, in a surprise attack on the Almohad caliph's army at Las Navas de Tolosa near Jaen in Andalusia on 16 July 1212, was followed not only by the overrunning of Andalusia by the Castilians, but also by the Portuguese advancing south to conquer the Algarve. The castle of Alcácer do Sal was successfully besieged in 1217.

Afonso's son, Sancho II (r. 1223–48), focused on territorial expansion against the Moors, capturing Sesimbra in 1236 and Silves in 1242. However, hostile nobles and clerics overthrew Sancho, with the crucial help of Pope Innocent IV, who ordered his removal in 1247. A civil war accompanied by Castilian intervention produced chaos, and Sancho died in exile in Spain in 1248, being succeeded by his brother Afonso, who had been called to the throne by some of the nobility in 1246. Afonso III (r. 1248–79) sought support by calling a *cortes* in 1254, the first attended by commoners, and also conquered the Algarve, capturing Faro, the last Moorish fortress, in 1249.

That, however, did not end conflict. The Marinid sultanate of Morocco, which had supplanted the Almohads in 1269, began attacking the Christian kingdoms in 1275 and had some successes. However, in 1340, Afonso IV of Portugal and his son-in-law Alfonso XI of Castile convincingly defeated Abu l-Hasan, the 'Black Sultan', at the battle of Río Salado near Tarifa. Most of the army was Castilian, but the Portuguese played a key role, defeating the forces from Granada. This decisive defeat led to the Marinids returning to North Africa. Afonso commissioned the

Padrão do Salado, a monument in Guimarães, to commemorate the sweeping victory.

Christianisation

Conquest saw Christianisation in conquered areas, notably with church building, as with the Romanesque cathedral at Braga. Many churches, for example the cathedral of Silves, which became a bishopric in 1253, were built on the same foundations as the mosques they replaced, which was an important part of the removal and reuse of the Muslim legacy. The church of *Santa Maria de Almacave* in Lamego was built in the twelfth century on the site of a Muslim cemetery. The church of St Peter at Lourosa incorporates Roman, Visigothic and Moorish remains. Moreover, Muslim baths, which fulfilled ritual as well as social functions, were built over. In areas that were already part of the Christian kingdoms in Iberia, there was an architectural celebration of victory, with churches built or extended. In response to his vow to the Virgin in 1147 to do so, if he was able to capture Santarém, Afonso I, in 1153, founded a major Cistercian monastery at Alcobaça, now a UNESCO World Heritage site.

Many Muslims had fled from the conquered territories, but others remained to till the soil, some of whom were forced into slavery. This quest for slaves was supplemented by raiding, especially into North Africa. However, the architectural aesthetics of the Islamic world were also adopted in many respects. Thus, the *Capela da Glória* in Braga Cathedral was painted in Moorish geometric motifs in the sixteenth century.

Resettlement by Christians as Christian kingdoms expanded southward in Iberia was part of a longstanding process of growth and development through internal settlement. Migration and colonisation were key elements of policy. They drew on a broader process of population increase and agricultural development, but there were specific political aspects as authority was consolidated. This process included the establishment of towns, for example Sernancelhe in the tenth century. Moreover, military bases were designed to serve as governmental centres and economic nodes.

New monastic orders were a help to settlement, especially the Cistercians. The first Cistercian monastery in Portugal, that of St João de Tarouca, was founded in 1124. In the leafy Varosa Valley south of the Douro, it is now largely ruined, and certainly is not as preserved as the nearby Cistercian monasteries of Salzedas, founded in 1168. The Cistercians played a major role in introducing the Gothic to Portugal. Alongside significant transitional Romanesque-Gothic works, the Gothic style became important from the thirteenth century.

Other orders also founded monasteries, while the friars were responsible for foundations, such as the thirteenth-century Franciscan convent at Santarém. The foundations were confiscated in the nineteenth century, but their churches often survive separately, as in the Santa Clara Church in Oporto. Religious military orders, which gained, settled and protected extensive estates, were another help to settlement, notably the Order of the Templars, which existed in Portugal from 1128, that of the Hospitallers, the Order of Calatrava, a Castilian order, and that of Aviz, which was founded in 1146. These orders linked the Church and the aristocracy from which they recruited. Almourol, an island in the Tagus, is an attractive Templar site where the Moorish castle was rebuilt from 1171. The Templars were also given a large area in Beira Baixa in 1165 as a way to consolidate the Portuguese presence, and this led to the building of castles at Monsanto and Idanha-a-Velha in 1171.

Economic Expansion

Settlement responded to the environment, to economic possibilities and to the question of scale, and these variations produced a very diverse human geography in nearby settled areas. Further south, in the newly conquered regions, there were large, lightly populated areas and more Muslims. Large estates were created there, mostly to the benefit of the Church and the nobility. Most Christian peasants, however, remained further north. In that region, there was an intensification of settlement, not least with the rebuilding of existing sites. For example, churches were extended, with the chapel at Balsemão expanded in the fourteenth century.

Over the long term, from the tenth to the fourteenth centuries, agricultural prosperity was helped by a rising population, which provided markets and workers, as well as by improved technology including the introduction of windmills from the eleventh century. The wealthy, however, found it easier to benefit than independent peasant proprietors, many of whom were hit by problems and reduced to subordination.

Medieval Divisions

Aside from defending the country against Castile with new fortifications, for example at Valença do Minho and at Monção, Afonso III had to defend the conquest of the Algarve from Castilian claims, and succeeded in doing this by the Treaty of Badajoz of 1267. He also proved able to resist papal demands and thus offered an important assertion of sovereignty.

His successor, Denis (Dinis in Portuguese; r. 1279–1325), pushed through reform, including of the judicial system. A very cultured and learned individual, in 1290 he founded a university in Lisbon, which was finally established permanently in Coimbra in 1537. Denis also strengthened Portuguese government and the state, not least by a concordat with the Pope in 1289 that extended royal jurisdiction over Church property, by signing a treaty with England in 1308, and by building or strengthening fortifications on or near the frontier with Castile, as at Chaves, where only the keep survives, Beja, Castelo Mendo, Castelo Rodrigo, Estremoz, Linhares, Pinhel, Sabugal, Sortelha and Trancoso, where the town walls survive. Although not a warrior king, Denis took advantage of the death of Sancho IV of Castile in 1295 and fought the infant Ferdinand IV of Castile in 1295–7. In the Treaty of Alcanizes of 1297, Denis gave up some frontier villages, but gained Olivenza and confirmation of possession of the Algarve. The treaty also led to an alliance that kept the peace for forty years.

Denis's main residence was in the castle at Leiria, and a legacy from his reign was his major expansion of the *Pinhal de Leiria*, a pine forest on the coast that provided a barrier to the inward spread of the coastal dunes, and that also served as a source for timber for shipbuilding. His support for the economy was seen with his chartering of fairs which encouraged trade as well as agricultural production for the market. This helped increase the activity and goods subject to taxation. Denis was also responsible for the lower storey of the Cloister of Silence in the monastery at Alcobaça, and for the castle at Óbidos, a town he gave to his wife as a wedding gift. In response to the papal suppression of the Templar Order in 1312, Denis transformed it in Portugal into the Order of Our Lord Jesus Christ, which was founded in 1317. Its headquarters from 1356 were at Tomar and it played an important role in Portuguese history, notably when Henry the Navigator was its lay governor.

The economic, social and political situation became far more difficult subsequently, notably with the Black Death of 1348–50, which led to the death of about a third of the population. Land was abandoned, villages deserted and agricultural production fell, putting a strain on revenues. Social tensions rose markedly as landlords sought to increase their return from the now smaller workforce. Sheep-rearing, which required fewer workers, expanded, as in England, and produced benefits for those involved, principally major landowners.

Denis's son, Afonso IV (r. 1325–57), had difficult relations with Castile and these interacted with Portuguese court politics, as Afonso's heir, Peter, had a relationship with his wife's lady-in-waiting, Inês de Castro, a member of the Galician nobility with Castilian links. The death of his wife led in 1345 to Peter living openly with Inês and recognising all her children as his. Concerned about growing Castilian influence, Afonso ordered the murder of Inês in 1355. A furious Peter rebelled, only to be defeated. When, soon after, Peter succeeded to the throne as Peter I (r. 1357–67), he had two of the killers brought back from Spain and executed publicly in 1361; he ripped their hearts out. The story that Peter had Inês exhumed and crowned, and that he ordered the court to pay homage to her, only dates from 1577 and is probably a myth. They are buried facing each other in the monastery of Alcobaça so that they would see each other when reborn at the Last Judgment.

Peter's successor, Ferdinand I (r. 1367–83), claimed the Castilian throne in 1369, and this helped further to involve Portugal in the complex dynastic and domestic politics of Castile. Castilian forces burned and pillaged Lisbon in 1373. Ferdinand left no male heir and was succeeded not, as agreed in 1382, by his daughter Beatrice, the wife of John I of Castile, but by his illegitimate half-brother, John, after an interregnum in which John at first assassinated Count João Fernandes Andeiro, the Galician lover of Ferdinand's widow, Leonor, who had been left in charge. Similarly, Afonso I had needed in 1128 to defeat his mother Teresa and her lover, Count Fernão Peres de Trava of Galicia, who had dominated Portugal from 1121 until the defeat. Civil conflict in 1383–5 saw Leonor backed by much of the nobility and clergy and associated with Castilian control, while John relied on the support of the middling orders. Leonor was forced to abdicate from the regency by John I of Castile who invaded in 1384, besieging Lisbon without success.

The Foundation of the House of Aviz

In 1385, the *cortes*, the parliament, met at Coimbra and acclaimed John as King John I (r. 1385–1433), the first of the house of Aviz. In 1385, the Castilians attacked anew. A subsidiary force invaded the Minho, being defeated at Trancoso. John I of Castile with French help meanwhile advanced into central Portugal with a 31,000 strong army. He was defeated on 14 August 1385 at Aljubarrota. Two hundred English archers played a significant role in the battle, which, by extension was part both of the Hundred Years War between England and France (1337–1453), and of the dynastic politics and warfare by which John, Duke of Lancaster, a younger son of Edward III of England, sought to establish his family on the throne of Castile. The 6600-strong Portuguese force defeated the Castilians, with heavy losses for the latter.

This major battle can be well understood thanks to an interpretative centre on the battlefield near Batalha (battle), where a dramatic monastery, *Santa Maria da Vitória*, was built in 1388–1434, in fulfilment to John I of Portugal's vow to the Virgin Mary to do so in return for his victory. The Gothic interior holds the tombs of John, his English wife, Philippa of Lancaster (Queen 1387–1415), a daughter of John of Gaunt, and four of their six sons, the 'Illustrious Generation', including Henry the Navigator, whose alleged birthplace in 1394 can be visited in the *Casa do Infante* in Oporto. Building on the Anglo-Portuguese treaty of 1373, which established a perpetual friendship, the Treaty of Windsor of 1386, a pact of mutual support, launched a period of continuous alliance between England and Portugal. This was reinforced in later treaties, notably in 1654, 1660, 1661, 1703, 1815 and 1899, although the alliance clearly lapsed during the period of Spanish kings from 1580 to 1640. In 1943, Winston Churchill referred to the 1373 treaty when announcing the granting to Britain of base rights in the Azores.

After her marriage at Oporto, Philippa had John's mistress banished from court to a convent where she became the prioress. Other royal wives were to have a similar problem, including those of John V and Joseph I. Influential at court, Philippa backed the scheme to conquer Ceuta.

Victory at Aljubarrota in 1385 was followed by the retreat of the Castilian army, and by the aristocracy rallying round John, who won a further victory at Valverde in Castile later that year. The Portuguese towns still held by the Castilians surrendered. John I of Castile's death in 1390 guaranteed peace. The opposition between Portugal and Castile, and their alignment respectively with England and France, ensured that the two backed rival popes during the Great Schism, which, in turn, exacerbated differences.

The warfare of the period helped ensure that many of the fortifications from the medieval period were directed against invasion from Castile or civil war, rather than against the Moors. Thus, in 1356–76, Oporto received impressive new walls. The Gothic cloister in its cathedral also dates from the fourteenth century. John moreover greatly strengthened the castle at Bragança. In Sintra, he rebuilt a palace on a Moorish fort.

Meanwhile, the key monument to late medieval Portugal remains Batalha, where the monastery was followed from about 1430 by sumptuous cloisters, which included a series of royal mortuary chapels. However, they remain unfinished because Manuel I (r. 1495–1521), great-grandson of John I of Portugal, moved instead to found a large new monastery at Jerónimos near the Tagus coast at Belém. Commissioned around 1501, this represented a major shift in the focus of Portuguese attention towards the oceans.

A key consolidator of Portuguese power and the longest reigning of all Portuguese rulers, John not only founded the royal house of Aviz, but also was the progenitor of that of Braganza (Bragança in Portuguese) because his illegitimate son became, in 1443, Afonso (1377–1461), the first Duke of Braganza. His mother, Inês Pires, has been variously described as the daughter of a Jewish cobbler and, alternatively, a member of a noble family.

John I's legacy could not prevent a civil war in 1449 as a result of tensions within the royal family following the regency for Afonso V (r. 1438–81), who had come to the throne after Duarte (r. 1433–8) died of the plague, as his father John I had done before him. This premature death led to divisions over the regency, notably between Duarte's unpopular foreign wife, Eleanor of Aragón, who was backed by the nobility, and John's son, Peter, Duke of Coimbra, who was supported by the *cortes* and became regent. In the civil war of 1449, Afonso, who was heavily influenced by Afonso, Duke of Braganza, turned on his uncle, Peter, who was defeated and killed during the battle of Alfarrobeira. This was the relatively short Portuguese version of the English Wars of the Roses.

John I, meanwhile, had seized Ceuta back in 1415, launching Portugal on a course of African expansion. The sea was seen as linking, not dividing. In part, there was a defensive fear that the Moors would strike back by sea, as they had done since 711, but there was also the ambition to take forward the process of driving them back, and notably so in competition with Castile.

5. The Age of Expansion, 1415–1580

The Portuguese and Africa

Portugal had long engaged with the sea, notably because of the importance of fishing. Thanks to its position and this history, it was to be Portugal, and not Spain, that first took forward the Atlantic potential of the Iberian peninsula. Portugal intervened in Morocco, where Ceuta was captured in 1415, and defeated a counterattack there in 1419. In 1418, Pope Martin V issued a papal bull confirming to Portugal the lands conquered from the Moors. Portugal also became an expansionist maritime power along, and off, the north-western coast of Africa. Portuguese settlement of Madeira began about 1420, of the Azores in 1439 and of the Cape Verde Islands in 1462; they had been discovered by the Portuguese in 1419, around 1427 and 1456 respectively. They were all uninhabited.

In the 1440s, after Gil Eanes had rounded the stormy Cape Bojador in 1434, proving it was safe to do so, as had been doubted, the Portuguese explored the African coast as far as modern Guinea. Cape Blanco was reached in 1441, and the peninsula of Cabo Verde (Cape Verde, Cap-Vert) in modern Senegal rounded in 1444. As a result, the Portuguese, searching for the legendary *Rio do Ouro* (River of Gold), had got past the Sahara and reached the far-more inhabited West Africa.

The Portuguese discovered early on that slave raiding met strong resistance from the coastal kingdoms south of the Senegal river, many of which were far from weak. Instead, trade was a more successful means of access and helped to finance further

Henry the Navigator (1394–1460)

The third son of John I, and a key figure in Portugal's overseas expansion, Henry did not actually sail forth further than the capture of Ceuta in Morocco. Instead, in part in order to pursue conflict with the Moors, Henry exploited his control over the Order of Christ as lay governor of the order to finance exploration and also tried to focus on navigational expertise to aid that goal. The navigation school Henry reputably founded at Sagres may be myth, in as much as no evidence of a physical building or teaching staff has been found. However, there was a 'school' in the sense of a collected body of navigational knowledge. Under Henry, the Portuguese discovered the pattern of Atlantic trade winds. Having encouraged the capture of Ceuta in 1415, Henry sought, with the help of his brother Duarte (r. 1433–8), to find the West African sources of the caravans that brought gold there. Deeply religious and interested in freeing the Holy Land, he was a celibate. Henry died in debt. 'The Navigator' was a later title.

Henry the Navigator, his nephew Afonso V (r. 1438–81) and his great-nephew John II (r. 1481–95) all appear in the *Adoration of St Vincent*, an altarpiece painted in about 1467–70, generally believed to be by Nuno Gonçalves, and held in the national museum of art (*Museu Nacional de Arte Antiga*) in Lisbon. The brilliantly coloured painting, a polyptych, includes a range of society, both secular and spiritual, from the great to the humble (a fisherman, a friar, and a beggar). St Vincent is featured.

expansion. The Portuguese presence along the West African coast served to divert the gold and other valuables of central West Africa towards coastal entrepôts, rather than across the Sahara to North Africa. In 1452, the gold from West Africa meant that it was possible to mint the first gold *cruzado* coins.

In the second half of the fifteenth century, the Portuguese then pushed south. Afonso V (r. 1438–81), who was known as 'the African' because of his expansionism in Morocco, was, in 1471, the first Portuguese king to call himself 'King of Portugal and the Algarves', rather than the Algarve, as the territories added in Africa came to be regarded as possessions of the kingdom of the Algarve. The Algarves were thought of as the southern Portuguese territories, whether in Europe or in Africa. Under Afonso, Portugal was active in conquest in Morocco, but he did not pursue Henry the Navigator's work after the death of his uncle in 1460.

His son, John II (r. 1481–95) was far more active. The profits from the trading base of São Jorge da Mina, founded in 1482, financed later voyages, such as those of Diogo Cão and Bartolomeu Dias. Mina itself was a logistical achievement, prefabricated with stones, timbers and tiles all prepared in Portugal. The islands of Fernando Pó, Príncipe, São Tomé and Ano Bom were discovered and claimed in 1483. Further south, a presence was established on the coast of what became Angola. Conflict and trade, however, were not the sole relationships. In 1483, Cão became the first European to set foot in the kingdom of Kongo. Peaceful relations were established and, in 1491, the King was baptised as John I. A blend of Christianity and local religious elements spread readily. Cão died on his second voyage about 1486. Subsequently, Portuguese explorers rounded the Cape of Good Hope at the southern limit of Africa, Dias leading the way.

Initially, the Portuguese did not rely solely on state activity. Thus, the presence on the Gold Coast began with the discovery of Mina in 1469 by the sea captains of Fernão Gomes, a wealthy financier. However, the Portuguese state soon came to play a much greater role and Mina's gold trade was controlled as a royal monopoly.

Drawing on recent developments in ship construction and navigation, specifically the fusion of Atlantic and Mediterranean techniques of hull construction and lateen and square-rigging, as well as on advances in location finding at sea, the Portuguese enjoyed advantages over other vessels, whether the latter carried cannon or not. Developments in rigging permitted them greater speed, improved manoeuvrability and a better ability to sail close to the wind; although the wind dropping could be a major problem in conflict against galleys.

Information also played a major role in Portuguese effectiveness. Thanks to the use of the compass and other developments in navigation, it was possible to chart the sea and to assemble knowledge about it, and, therefore, to have greater control over the relationship between the enormity of the ocean and the transience of man than ever before. The Portuguese made a major effort to accumulate information that would aid navigation, and also to keep it secret from rivals. They had also built up a pool of experienced seamen during the fifteenth century, seamen who were able to exploit the technological advances to maximum effect.

The Portuguese and the Indian Ocean

Pêro da Covilhã, a Portuguese explorer and secret agent, sailed down the Red Sea in 1487 and, from there, first to India and then to the east coast of Africa, as far as Sofala in modern Mozambique (1489). He was following a route dependent on Islamic powers. Not so for Bartolomeu Dias, who rounded the Cape of Good Hope in January 1488, without seeing it, and entered the Indian Ocean. A squire of the royal court, Dias was instructed to find the dominions of Prester John. He reached the mouth of the

Boesmans River where his crew forced him to abandon his plan to sail to India. What he originally called the Cape of Storms was renamed by John II the Cape of Good Hope. Dias was sunk off the Cape in 1500 in a storm on his second voyage.

Portuguese warships were more heavily gunned than those of their opponents. Arriving in Indian waters in 1498, Vasco da Gama dropped anchor near the port of Calicut in Kerala on 20 May, with vessels carrying cannon that Asian warships could not resist successfully in battle. The Portuguese were seeking trade, but their arrival disrupted established trading relationships, leading to conflict. A model of his flagship, the *São Gabriel*, can be seen in the maritime museum in Faro.

The technological gap in their favour helped give the Portuguese victory over the Calicut fleet in 1502, despite the latter being supported by Arab vessels. In the battle, Portuguese gunfire, especially the heavy guns carried close to the waterline, saw off boarding attempts and thus countered their opponents' numerical advantage. The Mamluks of Egypt then intervened against the Portuguese, as part of a range of opposition Spain did not face in the Americas. The Mamluks were successful at first but, in 1509, the Egyptian fleet was largely destroyed by the Portuguese off Diu, also on the west coast of India. That year, a Portuguese expedition under Diogo Lopes de Sequeira sailed east from India, reaching Malacca. It was not to be the limit of Portuguese exploration.

The Portuguese initially relied on the caravel, a swift, seaworthy but relatively small ship, ideal for coastal exploration and navigation, as well as the *nau* or 'great ship', a very large carrack-type vessel. There is a replica of a *nau* moored opposite the shipbuilding museum in Vila do Conde, as well as models and relevant exhibits. They then developed the galleon as a vessel able to sail great distances. It was longer and narrower than earlier carracks, with a reduced hull width-to-length ratio, and was faster, more manoeuvrable and capable of carrying a heavier armament.

The Portuguese brought galleons into the Indian Ocean from the mid-1510s, while continuing to use their large carracks to transport goods back to Portugal from the Indies. As early as 1518, the standard armament of a Portuguese galleon was thirty-five guns. Effectiveness in hand-to-hand conflict was also important: cannon alone were not what led to victory. In India, the fleets of Jepara and Gujarat were defeated in 1513 and 1528 respectively.

Another key element in Portuguese expansion was their string of fortified naval bases. Their model was the Venetian *Stato da Mar* in the Mediterranean: a chain of islands and fortresses protecting entrepôts, and enforcing a monopolistic or near-monopolistic trading position. Portuguese sailors knew that they could replenish in safety at a series of 'way stations', such as Luanda and Mozambique, on their long voyages to and from Asia. Naval power thus provided a cover for the spread of Portuguese bases which, in turn, supported the Portuguese military and commercial systems. These bases could be attacked by local rulers, as were Chaul and Goa in India in 1571, but, without naval strength, it was not possible to cut the bases off from relief by sea, which proved crucial in these cases.

Having entered the Indian Ocean, Portugal established bases on the east coast of Africa, notably at Kilwa (1505), Mombasa (1505), Sofala (1505), Mozambique (1507), Malindi (1520), Pemba (1520) and Delagoa Bay (1544). So also on the west coast of India, including Cochin (1503), Cannanore (1505), Anjediva (1505), Chaul (1509), Goa (1510), Quilon (1512), Mumbai (1530), Diu (1535), Surat (1540) and Damão (1558). In the Persian Gulf, there were bases at Bandar Abbas (1507), Bahrain (1515), Hormuz (1515) and Muscat (1550), the last two providing a strong position at the mouth of the Gulf. Indeed, John III (r. 1521–57) was called 'The Coloniser'.

The complex role of local politics was amply displayed in Ceylon (Sri Lanka), where the Portuguese had first landed in 1505, signing a trade treaty with the kingdom of Kotte on the south-west coast. King Dharmapala of Kotte became a vassal of the Portuguese crown in 1551, and in 1580 agreed to leave the kingdom to Portugal when he died. However, by the 1590s, when he did so, the inland kingdom of Udarata had claimed rule over the entire island and was fighting to expel the Portuguese. The situation in Ceylon showed both that alliance with local rulers could be a valuable asset and that it could be unstable. The same was to be true of Portuguese cooperation with Iran where, initially, the Safavids accepted the Portuguese position in Hormuz, which was far from their centres of power and concern. Meanwhile the Portuguese provided cannon to the Safavids who used it against the Ottomans (Turks) and the Uzbeks. In 1535, the Portuguese were able to build a fort at Diu because Bahadur Shah of Gujarat, whose navy they had defeated in 1528, was by then seeking their aid against Mughal expansion.

Cooperation based on strength also helped the Portuguese in East Africa, with the ruler of Malindi assisting in capturing Mombasa in 1589 and becoming sheikh there, while the Portuguese built a powerful fortress.

Further east, the Portuguese established themselves in the major commercial and Islamic centre of Malacca. The city had numerous bronze cannon but, in 1511, the Portuguese cannon proved superior, while a well-coordinated and determined Portuguese force, reliant on pikes as much as firepower, defeated the sultan's war elephants.

The Portuguese came into the Indian Ocean more to trade than to conquer. Violence was employed in order to influence or even dictate the terms of trade, in particular by excluding rivals, rather than to gain territory. The Portuguese lacked the manpower to become a major Asian territorial power. The population of Portugal – about one million – was not large, and there were many other emigration opportunities, especially to less remote Brazil. Tropical diseases killed many of the Portuguese who went to India, and there was a shortage of female emigrants.

In the East Indies, fortified posts were established in Ternate (1522), Solor (1562) and Tidore (1578), giving the Portuguese direct access to spice production there. John III's role in the spice trade also led to his being called the 'Pepper King'.

Commercial bases, rather than fortified positions, were established at Macao in China (1557) and Nagasaki in Japan (1570). Trade had many meanings as a Japanese account of Portuguese slave trading in the 1580s reveals:

> They buy several hundred men and women and take them aboard their black ships. They place chains on their hands and feet and throw them into the holds of their ships. Their torments are worse than those in hell . . . It is said that hell has been made manifest on earth. We hear that the local Japanese have learned their ways by imitating them and sell their own children, parents, wives and daughters.

In 1518, Pedro Reinel, the leading Portuguese chart-maker with official status, was responsible for a map of the Indian Ocean in which he drew on the 1511 expedition to Java and the Moluccas. Portuguese expeditions to these waters produced their own information and obtained copies of charts from native pilots. The charts of the Indian Ocean made by Sebastião Lopes in his portolan atlas of about 1565 reflected a growing awareness of the coastline, for example of Sumatra. Moreover, as an instance of the growing multi-centred nature of the empire, Goa developed as a centre of Portuguese mapmaking.

En route to the Indian Ocean, a Portuguese expedition under Pedro Álvares Cabral 'discovered' Brazil in 1500. It was initially called *Vera Cruz* (True Cross) or *Terra dos Papagaios* (Parrot-land). In *The Adoration of the Magi*, painted around 1503–5 by Vasco Fernandes – known as Grão Vasco (the Great Vasco) – and held in the museum of his work in Viseu, a Brazilian Indian is depicted as one of the three kings. Nevertheless, Brazil was not actively developed by the Portuguese until the 1530s, and then largely in response to incursions by French seamen. The Portuguese made only slow progress at the expense of the Tupinambá and Tapuya, with their muskets of little value against mobile warriors who were expert archers and well-adapted to forest warfare. However, the Portuguese were helped by rivalries between tribes and the alliance of some. São Paulo was established in 1532, the year in which the colony was organised under captaincies (provinces). Bahia became the capital in 1549 and Rio de Janeiro was founded in 1565.

Despite the exploration of the coast of north-east North America, and notably of Labrador, by João Fernandes Lavrador and Pêro de Barcelos in 1498, Portugal did not have a territorial impact further north in the New World. However, its fishing ensured that it was important. This was particularly so on the Grand Banks off Newfoundland where Portuguese fishermen found cod in great quantities and salted it for sale in Portugal. This brought prosperity to a number of ports, notably Aveiro, where there were important salt pans. However, in 1575, a storm created a sand bar that blocked the harbour. In nearby Ílhavo, there is a maritime museum.

Not all the Portuguese targets fell. In 1510, Calicut in India was attacked by Fernando Coutinho, who was defeated and killed. In particular, the attempt to advance into the Red Sea failed, which was important as the Red Sea was the primary route for Islamic naval counterattack into the Indian Ocean. Had the Portuguese been successful in seizing Mecca and Medina, it would have won great prestige and helped to advance the cause of the recapture of Jerusalem. However, having succeeded at Goa (1510) and Malacca (1511), Afonso de Albuquerque, the Viceroy of the Indies from 1509 to 1515, failed at Aden in 1513. The Portuguese also failed at Aden and Jeddah in 1517, and at Suez in 1541; although, under pressure, in 1529, the Emir of Aden agreed to become a Portuguese vassal.

Christian Expansion

Christian expansion was a major theme, one pushed within Portugal and outside. Henry the Navigator was deeply religious, as was Afonso V, who had planned a pilgrimage to the Holy Land, and Manuel I. In 1455, a papal bull awarded Portugal what it 'discovered' in Africa with the exception of the lands that belonged to Prester John. The Portuguese initially vindicated their arrival in India from 1498 by drawing on the legacy of the Apostle Thomas. His relics were discovered, allegedly, while the presence of local Christians apparently meant that the Crown was reaching out to free them from oppression and to gather in all Christians under the papacy. At Cochin in Kerala, there are sites that recall this history.

Portugal played the key role on another developing religious frontier between Christendom and Islam: Portuguese musketeers sent in 1541 helped Christian Abyssinia resist attack from the expansionist Islamic sultanate of Adal in the early 1540s. Moreover, Ottoman (Turkish) attacks on Diu in 1538, Hormuz in 1552 and the Swahili coast of Africa in 1593 were all repulsed. The Ottomans entered the Indian Ocean, once they had overcome Mamluk Egypt in 1517, to protect the position of the latter in the Red Sea that they had taken over, and then to drive the Portuguese out. Although the Portuguese ally in Aden was killed and it was captured in 1538, the Ottomans found they were unable to sustain a more far-flung presence. Instead, it was Portugal that did so and at a much greater range. Ottoman plans of joining with Aceh, Portugal's Islamic opponent in northern Sumatra, were among the many Ottoman schemes that proved abortive.

The emphasis on religion was important. Both Portugal and Spain put great stress on their roles as defenders of the faith. This linked their positions domestically, within Christendom, and further afield. In the first case, there was no tolerance for

Protestantism and an increasingly harsh attitude to Jews and Muslims. Having, in response to Spanish pressure, expelled Jews in 1497, Manuel demanded that those who stayed in Portugal convert to Christianity. They became the *conversos*.

The process was violent. There was a bloody pogrom in 1506. Synagogues were seized, that at Tomar becoming a prison and later a chapel. It now holds a Jewish museum. In Oporto, the church of São João Novo was built in 1539 on land that had been part of the Jewish quarter. The narrow lanes of the area also derive from that quarter. The surviving remains of the Jewish quarter in Bragança date from this era. Many of those who fled went to France and the Netherlands, notably Amsterdam.

The Inquisition came to play a major role from 1536 as part of strengthened relations with the papacy under John III (r. 1521–57). Proclamations issued that year invited accusations against those suspected of being a heretic, with a penalty of imprisonment if information was later found to have been withheld. As 'New Christians' had to baptise their children, so it was possible to accuse them of apostasy and heresy. Signs of false conversion by those the Inquisition referred to as Judaisers were listed as including wearing white or dressing smartly on a Saturday, cleaning or sweeping the house on a Friday, and not eating pork, fish with skin and rabbit. Jews who would not convert risked being burned alive after a trial that generally followed torture. Few were acquitted, but secret practice in remote areas, notably in the far north, ensured that Judaism continued. The Inquisition has left its mark on place names, notably with the *Pátio da Inquisição* in Coimbra. In Lisbon, heretics were burned to death in the *Terreiro do Paço* and in Rossio Square, which was next door to the headquarters of the Inquisition.

Abroad, the Portuguese supported proselytism in their colonies. The Jesuits played a prominent role there, as with the church built in São Paulo in 1554. They were also significant church builders back in Portugal, as with the new cathedral founded in Coimbra in 1598, a building decorated with images of Jesuit saints.

The triumph of Portugal's role can be seen most vividly in the luxuriant Jerónimos monastery at Belém, west of Lisbon, built between 1502 and 1572. This was a large monastic complex dependent on a tripartite hall church. Commissioned by Manuel to commemorate the new route to the Indies, the church includes the tombs of Vasco da Gama and of Luís Vaz de Camões. The poet celebrated da Gama in his epic *Os Lusíadas* (*The Lusiads*), an account, published in 1572, of the travails and triumphs of the explorers which has an iconic weight comparable to Cervantes and Shakespeare, as well as heady language. The exotic cloisters at the Jerónimos monastery are entrancing and also present the symbolism of the Age of Discovery, with the armillary sphere, a navigational device associated with Manuel, and the cross of the Order of Christ, the military order that financed some of the voyages. The motifs of Renaissance Classicism characterise much of the decoration.

Nearby, the Tower of Belém, jutting out into the Tagus, was designed to help defend the harbour of Lisbon from attack from the Atlantic. A stone rhinoceros represents the live one sent to Pope Leo X in 1515 by Manuel.

The Manueline architecture of these works reflects a sense of confidence as well as the wealth that financed a range of activity. Other major works include parts of the Templar complex at Tomar, notably the upper choir in the church, the interior of the *Igreja de Jesus* at Setúbal, and the roof towers and altarpiece of the cathedral of Braga. The Manueline chapterhouse of the monastery of Santa Cruz in Coimbra has a frieze focused on exploration. In the sixteenth-century Misericórdia church in Oporto, the painting *Fons Vitae* (*Fountain of Life*) shows Manuel and his family around a fountain of blood from the crucified Christ. Major artists of the period include the Viseu painter Vasco

Fernandes (c. 1475–c. 1542). Five of the twenty works he painted in 1506–11 for the apse of the cathedral of Lamego survive in the museum there in the old episcopal palace, and their realism and wonderful colours radiate quality. A museum of his paintings can be found in Viseu. It illustrates the influence of the Flemish painters of the Northern Renaissance, notably in naturalism and the use of light.

The Manueline, very much a last flurry of the Gothic, was followed, under John III, by the more restrained Renaissance style. It is important not to read a wider meaning too easily from this change, but this restraint accorded with a measure of retrenchment under John, one seen in frugality and anti-sumptuary legislation as well as his favour for the Inquisition. Ornamentation became less significant in architecture. However, the Manueline style was revived with neo-Manueline architectural features in the late nineteenth century, for example the Pena Palace, notably with the Triton Arch and the Arab Room.

An exemplary history, meanwhile, was offered. Manuel commissioned from the historian Duarte Galvão *Crónica de El-Rei D. Afonso Henriques*, the life and deeds of Portugal's first king. Finished in 1505, this work dealt with the victory at Ourique over the Moors in 1139, as well as the capture of Lisbon from the Moors in 1147. The role of the Crown as the traditional protector of the Christian faith was therefore made clear, with success vindicating this role. This interpretation was significant as a justification for Portugal's overseas expansion at that juncture, and also in the competition for prestige with neighbouring Spain – not least prestige as the defender of Christendom at a time when the papacy was arbitrating between Spain and Portugal over transoceanic territorial claims. Galvão prefigured Camões as an account of exemplary and expansionist heroism.

Support for the Church included having Évora elevated to an archbishopric in 1544 and ensuring that the Algarve was transferred from the Spanish archdiocese of Seville. Évora also gained a university in 1550. In 1573, King Sebastian was to order the construction of the Royal Basilica in Castro Verde to commemorate victory at Ourique.

Politics in the Peninsula

Eased relations with Castile helped greatly in Portuguese expansionism. Initially, on a long-established pattern, relations were poor. Indeed, Portugal and Castile fought in a war of the Castilian succession in 1475–9. The claims of Isabella, the half-sister of Henry IV of Castile (r. 1454–74), were contested by her half-niece, Joanna la Beltraneja, the possibly illegitimate daughter of Henry. Isabella was backed by Aragón (she was married to its heir apparent, Ferdinand, her cousin), and Joanna by Portugal. She was married to her uncle, Afonso V, who proclaimed himself king of Castile and León. The aristocracy was divided. The succession was decided in favour of Isabella by battle. Afonso nearly bankrupted Portugal.

Thereafter, relations improved and, outside Europe, the two powers were able to agree. In 1479, by the Treaty of Alcáçovas, Castile surrendered claims to trading rights in Guinea and the Gold Coast to Portugal. This agreement, confirmed by a papal bull in 1481, was a reflection of the longstanding Spanish willingness to purchase slaves from others, and looked toward the sanctioned division of the newly 'discovered' lands between Spanish and Portuguese zones by the Treaty of Tordesillas of 1494 along a meridian 370 leagues west of the Cape Verde islands, a treaty correcting the 1493 bull of Pope Alexander VI that had been more favourable to Castile. John II (r. 1481–95) used the threat of force to secure this revision. This division awarded the lands to the east to Portugal and those to the west to Castile. Africa, the Indian Ocean and what was later 'discovered' as Brazil in effect were awarded to Portugal. Relations had been eased because John had turned away from Castilian ambitions in order to focus on African expansion.

John's son, Afonso, died aged sixteen in 1491, in a horse-riding accident on the banks of the Tagus, but it was rumoured that he had been murdered by Spanish agents concerned about his claim on the Spanish inheritance through his marriage with Isabella, daughter of Ferdinand of Aragón and Isabella of Castile. John, having, in the face of opposition by his wife and the rulers of Spain, failed to legitimate his illegitimate son, George, Duke of Coimbra, left his throne to his cousin and brother-in-law, Manuel, Duke of Beja, who became Manuel I (r. 1495–1521). Manuel's older brother, Diogo, Duke of Viseu, had been stabbed to death in 1484 by John II who sought to limit the powers of the greater nobility. John had already had Duke Ferdinand II of Braganza beheaded in 1483 in Évora, near the centre of the Duke's power, on the charge of treason.

The Treaty of Saragossa (1529) provided a corresponding line of delimitation in East Asia to that of Tordesillas, so as to settle Portugal and Spain's respective interests and to clarify zones of expansion. This process dramatically reduced the potential risk and cost of Portuguese activity. That outcome was further secured by dynastic marriages between the Portuguese royal family and the Habsburgs. Manuel married Prince Afonso's widow Isabella in 1497, while Manuel I's son, John III (r. 1521–57), married Catherine of Austria in 1525; Manuel's daughter, Isabella, married Charles V in 1526, which played a key role in Philip II of Spain's eventual claim to the Portuguese throne; and John's daughter, Maria Manuela, married the future Philip II in 1543. The contrast between the good relations of Portugal and Spain in much of the sixteenth century and difficult ones earlier and later were significant.

Portugal's role in the Indies brought both wealth to Portugal and a strong sense of mission, the two fused in the construction of splendid churches. The 'royal fifth' (a 20 per cent tax on precious metals and commodities, including slaves) ensured that trade led to great wealth for the monarchy. This process was encouraged by the degree to which it was relatively easy to control the trade which set out from and ended in Lisbon. Oporto and the ports of the Algarve did not share this role. Established within the royal palace on the riverbank at Lisbon, the *Casa da India* and the *Casa da Guiné e da Mina* were part of a state monopoly run by the same director and had several treasuries and administrators. These offices supervised the loading and unloading, and dealt with all commercial matters relating to contracts, dues and so on. The *Armazém da Guiné e Indias* (Storehouse of Guinea and the Indies), the naval arsenal, dealt with nautical issues from the dockyards to the supply of marine charts. Within this, the hydrographic office was responsible for securing the return of charts issued to pilots. In order to improve accuracy, returning pilots were expected to submit their charts and logbooks for scrutiny.

Alongside the wealth for the Crown, there was also prosperity for some of the explorers. Those who survived and prospered acquired land and built splendid houses. They also left tombs, such as that of Diogo de Azambuja in Montemor-o-Velho. Empire and trade brought wealth and activity across the country as well as ensuring that the streets of Lisbon became even more cosmopolitan with Africans eventually joined by South Asians and Brazilians. Shipbuilding developed, for example in Vila do Conde.

Transoceanic expansion provided particular opportunities for the bold. In the 1590s, Diego Veloso, a Portuguese mercenary, attempted to seize control of Cambodia, only to be overthrown in 1599. That year, Filipe de Brito, a Portuguese adventurer who had entered the service of the King of Arakan, became governor of Thanlyin (Syriam). He won independence, was awarded recognition by Portugal in 1602, and held control until the Burmese successfully besieged Thanlyin in 1613. Brito was impaled.

The Father of Portuguese Drama

Born possibly in Guimarães, the playwright Gil Vicente (*c.* 1465–*c.* 1536) was linked to the courts of Manuel I and John III and benefited from the patronage of Leonor, widow of John II. His first work, performed in 1502, was inspired by the Adoration of the Shepherds. Actor and author, he produced court plays until 1536. Alongside religious plays, he wrote comedies and tragicomedies. Human flaws are satirised, including the flaws of social groups. The first edition of his complete works was published in Lisbon in 1561–2, but the Inquisition sought to limit his influence.

Failure in Sub-Saharan Africa

Portugal, meanwhile, had also pursued expansion in Africa. This involved the settlement of coastal positions but unsuccessful campaigning in the interiors of Mozambique and Angola. In each, the Portuguese came up against impressive defenders and a difficult environment. Portuguese cannon proved to have little impact on African earthwork fortifications, while the slow rate of fire of muskets and the openness of African fighting formations reduced the effectiveness of firearms, and the Portuguese were successful only when supported by local troops.

In Angola, where, in 1575, the Portuguese established a base at Luanda, the only natural port on that part of the Atlantic coast and one where there were no other European bases, they entered into an alliance with the inland kingdom of Ndongo and, when expelled from there with heavy losses in 1579, employed their existing alliance with the kingdom of Kongo to advance on Ndongo in 1580, only to be defeated. Thereafter, the Portuguese used their Kongo alliance and their naval power on the River Kwanza to persuade a number of local rulers to switch from Ndongo to alliance with the Portuguese. With their help, a Ndongo force was defeated at Massangano in 1582. A full-scale attack on Ndongo's core region was mounted in 1590, but the Portuguese force was totally defeated near the River Lukala, leading to the collapse of the Portuguese alliance system. A peace negotiated in 1599 left the Portuguese largely confined to the coast. The Portuguese role in the fighting in part rested on firearms, but their skill as swordsmen was probably more significant and, in battle, they formed a heavy infantry core with local archers deployed on the flanks.

Disease was a real problem and notably so in the Zambezi Valley. An expedition of 700 musketeers sent in 1571–3 to the valley to seize the gold of Mutapa lost most of its men to disease and no gold mines were discovered. Disease killed both men and horses, the latter affecting the possibility of deploying cavalry. About 60 per cent of the Portuguese soldiers who served in Angola in 1575–90 died of disease. Most of the rest were killed or deserted.

The Portuguese had explicitly sought to emulate the achievement of the Spaniards in the New World. Instead, they revealed the total ineffectiveness of the European military system in land-based campaigns in sub-Saharan Africa. The environment was much more savage than the New World. Whereas Mexico and Peru were populous and had a well-developed agricultural system that could provide plenty of resources for an invader, Africa lacked comparable storehouses, food for plunder and roads. Mexico and Peru were also more centralised politically, and thus easier to take over once the ruler had been seized. Not so for most of Africa. The Portuguese also found the Africans well-armed, with well-worked iron weapons as good in some ways as the Portuguese steel weaponry and certainly better than the wood and obsidian of the New World.

Disaster in Morocco

The key failure, however, was in Morocco. Campaigning there was a reminder that the Portuguese did not see the ocean as a boundary, although proximity did play a key element. Far more Portuguese efforts were devoted to Morocco than to the Indian Ocean, but it is the latter that bulks larger in the historical record. There were twenty ships on Vasco da Gama's second voyage to India in 1502, while Afonso de Albuquerque wanted a large fleet manned by 3000 Portuguese, and attacked Aden in 1513 with 1000 Portuguese and 700 Malabar archers. In contrast, although the figures were probably exaggerated, the Portuguese allegedly used 400 ships and 30,000 men to capture Arzila on the Moroccan coast in 1471. With strong support from Afonso V (r. 1438–81), who was nicknamed *Africano*, Portuguese forces also took Alcácer in 1458, Larache and Tangier in 1471 (after failures to capture Tangier in 1437, 1463 and 1464), Agadir in 1505, Safi in 1508, Azamor in 1513 and Mazagão in 1514, gaining control of most of the towns on Morocco's Atlantic coast. The Portuguese thus sought to seize the trade of the region and to control the interior by dominating the coast.

The Portuguese were superior not only in the numbers and quality of their guns, but also in tactical expertise. However, a major change in Morocco then transformed the situation. The Wattasids of Fez were driven from much of Morocco by more vigorous opponents, the Sa'dis, and the latter improved their army, integrating arquebusiers and field artillery into their forces and developing combined infantry–cavalry tactics for their battles. Moreover, their light cavalry was more flexible than the heavier Portuguese cavalry. The Sa'dis captured Agadir in 1541, and the Portuguese were driven to abandon Safi (1542), Azamor (1540) and Arzila (1549).

Born in 1554, Sebastian came to the throne in 1557 because of the premature death of his father, Prince John: indeed, Sebastian was born eighteen days after his father's death. Named Sebastian because he was born on the saint's day (20 January), he had a very religious upbringing and saw Morocco as a field for a crusade. Sebastian sought to benefit from divisions within Morocco. Muhammad al-Mutawakkil, the ruler, had been deposed by his Turkish-backed uncle, Abd al-Malik, in 1576, and had appealed for Sebastian's assistance. Hoping to establish a client ruler, the immature Sebastian in 1578 led his 17,000-strong army into the interior of Morocco against the advice of his commanders.

Heavily outnumbered and crucially short of cavalry, Sebastian believed that his infantry would successfully resist the Moroccan cavalry. He sought battle at al-Qasr-al-Kabir/Alcácer-Quibir (Battle of the Three Kings) on 4 August. Sebastian deployed his infantry units in a deep phalanx, with cavalry on the flanks and artillery in the front. The Moroccan army consisted of lines of arquebusiers, with cavalry, including mounted arquebusiers, in the rear and on the flank. The Moroccans opened the battle with harrying attacks by horse arquebusiers and the unsupported Portuguese artillery was overrun. The Portuguese infantry fought well, however, and pressed hard on the Moroccan infantry. A second Moroccan cavalry attack pushed back the Portuguese cavalry on both flanks, but the Moroccans again lost impetus. A renewed attack by the Portuguese infantry allowed a gap to open in their left flank, which the Moroccans exploited with great effect. The Moroccan horse arquebusiers then succeeded in destroying the cohesion of the Portuguese rear right flank, and Sebastian's army disintegrated. This was an even worse disaster than the expedition against Tangier in 1437 in which the Portuguese army was starved into surrender and made to promise to return Ceuta, a promise that had been broken. In 1578, the skilful, well-disciplined Moroccan force had won a crushing victory thanks to superior leadership and discipline, more flexible units and tactics, and the events of the battle. The King was killed and the entire army was killed or captured. Some of the captives took part in the successful Moroccan march across the Sahara and invasion of the Niger Valley in 1590-1.

Legends, however, of the survival of Sebastian in a cave and predictions of his return for long circulated in Portugal, for example in João de Castro's edition of Gonçalo Anes Bandarra's *Trovas*. What was termed Sebastianism led to prophecies of a *Quinto Império* or Fifth Empire, as with those associated with the priest António Vieira in the 1660s. These prophecies reflected a strong sense of failure and humiliation that was driven home by the unpopularity of Spanish rule from 1580. Overshadowed today by Portugal's success in becoming an imperial power from Brazil to the East Indies, failure in Morocco had brought Portugal's first golden age to an abrupt close.

6. Spanish Interlude, 1580–1640

Spanish Conquest

Alcácer-Quibir in 1578 led to the end of Portuguese independence two years later. Unmarried, Sebastian had no children. His successor, his great-uncle Henrique – Henry II (or Henry I if Henry, Count of Portugal and father of Afonso Henriques (Afonso I), is not referred to as Henry I) – was the fifth son of Manuel I and brother of John III, but he was elderly, ill, far from vigorous and, from 1545, a cardinal. An instance of the way in which the Church, like the military orders and the army, was widely used to provide a livelihood for spare brothers, Henry 'the Chaste' had successively been Archbishop of Braga, Évora and Lisbon. Childless, Henry sought release from his religious vows so that he could marry, but Pope Gregory XIII refused, unwilling to anger Philip II of Spain, who was the most prominent Counter-Reformation ruler. Henry died on 31 January 1580 on his sixty-eighth birthday, a very good age for the period, but without having appointed a successor.

The succession was disputed. Both Philip II, the uncle of Sebastian, and António, Prior of Crato, a grandson of Manuel I and the illegitimate son of Manuel's second son, had claims. There was also a Braganza claim on the inheritance, but John, the sixth duke, a claimant through his wife (daughter of the younger brother of John III) and through her mother, did not press the claim. António had been captured at Alcácer-Quibir but, benefiting from a failure to realise his financial value, ransomed himself. There was a precedent for such a succession, as

John I had become king in 1385, launching the house of Aviz, despite being illegitimate. However, António lacked much support from the nobility and higher clergy, many of whom had been bribed by Philip II. As with John I in 1385, António's support was more from the lower classes, both lay and clerical.

On 19 July 1580, António was proclaimed king at Santarém, but Spanish forces, 47,000 strong, under Fernando, 3rd Duke of Alba, an experienced and determined commander, had already invaded in June. Such a large force was available because in 1579 the Spanish forces in the Low Countries had been withdrawn as part of a peace agreement that turned out only to be temporary. Moreover, Philip could afford to pay for German and Italian mercenaries. This was one of the most successful campaigns of the century and one that contrasted with earlier Spanish attacks and with those in the seventeenth and eighteenth centuries. Alba, who captured the frontier fortress of Elvas without resistance on 18 June, advanced further into Portugal nine days later. He was supported by a fleet from Cádiz, which landed troops at Cascais. Setúbal fell on 18 July. The outnumbered Portuguese under António were heavily defeated at Alcântara on 25 August, Lisbon falling two days later after street-by-street fighting. Coimbra followed on 8 September. The defeated Portuguese fled to Oporto, but failed to rally support, and the city was captured on 24 October by a Spanish force under Don Sancho d'Avila, transported by sea.

Recognised as king by the *cortes* of Tomar, Philip was crowned Philip I of Portugal on 25 March 1581. António had fled to France with the Portuguese crown jewels. In return for the promise to cede Brazil, the French provided support for him, including about 6000 to 7000 troops, to establish himself in the Azores, which had a strategic position athwart maritime routes. However, after failure in 1581, Spanish expeditions in 1582 and 1583 brought this to an end, the Spaniards both defeating a larger French fleet off St Miguel on 26 July 1582 and making an opposed landing.

António fled to France again and then, fearing assassination by Spanish agents, to England. He died in Paris in 1595.

Portugal, one of the world's two leading transoceanic colonial empires, had been taken over by its rival empire, Spain, with relatively little fighting, an obvious contrast to the contest between Portugal and Islam. This outcome reflected the primacy of the dynastic theme in sixteenth-century European politics: the destruction and exhaustion of the house of Aviz, with the death of Sebastian, the death of Henry and the absence of effective claimants, entailed the end of a Portugal independent from foreign control. False-Sebastians were hunted down and killed by Spanish agents. Belief in them reflected the hope of returning independence to Portugal.

Spain was anyway far more powerful than Portugal which, with the *Casa da India* empty, was bankrupt. As in the 1890s, serious financial problems hit hard at Portugal's ability to maintain its interests. Indeed, in the late 1560s, operating from Mexico, the Spaniards established themselves in the Philippines, even though it was on the Portuguese side of the delimitation line agreed by the Treaty of Saragossa in 1529.

Portuguese navigators worked for Spain. Thus, Évora-born Pedro Fernandes de Queirós (1563–1614) was chief pilot in an unsuccessful voyage to colonise the Solomon Islands in 1595 and established a settlement in 1606 at Big Bay on the north side of the island of Espiritu Santo in modern Vanuatu. He named the entire island group *Australia del Espiritu Santo* as he believed he had arrived at *Terra Australis*, the Great Southern continent.

The process of dynastic takeover was eased by the willingness to maintain distinct institutions and separate practices and privileges, as also with Scotland and England in 1603 when James VI of Scotland became James I of England. No new state was created by the succession of Philip I, who remained in Lisbon until 1583. Instead, Portugal did not lose its independence in 1580. A legitimate candidate to the throne, Philip established a dual monarchy: two states under one king. It was only with time, and especially in the 1620s and 1630s under the Count-Duke of Olivares, the leading minister of Philip IV of Spain (Philip III of Portugal), that policy became increasingly 'Iberist'.

Under the terms agreed in 1581, the regency in Portugal had to be held by a Portuguese individual or by a member of the royal family. When in 1583 Philip left for Spain, he made his nephew, Cardinal Albert of Austria, his viceroy in Portugal. Albert, who was also appointed Papal Legate and Grand Inquisitor for Portugal, held the post until 1593. Clerics were viceroys in 1603–8, 1612–19 and 1633. As a variation on the regency stipulations, a governing junta was installed in 1593–1600 and 1621–32, in each case with prominent Portuguese members, including the Archbishop of Lisbon in the first and the Bishop of Coimbra in the second. Philip had established a Council of Portugal in Madrid in order to provide advice. This was on the pattern of conciliar government used by Philip.

There was no issue with difference in religion as when Sigismund III of Poland (r. 1587–1632) became king of Sweden in 1592, only to be deposed in 1599 after a civil war that began in 1597. Indeed, the period of the Spanish monarchy saw a revitalisation of the Portuguese church with the introduction of Italian-style reforms including a better trained and more attentive parochial clergy.

Philip is part of the sequence of Portuguese monarchs depicted in statue form in the arcaded gallery alongside the St Gonçalo church in Amarante, a gallery that commemorates those who ruled while the monastery was under construction. Elsewhere, however, the Spanish rulers are not so favoured. Thus, in the eighteenth-century bishop's garden in Castelo Branco, the statues of monarchs stand guard on the balustrades, but the Spanish monarchs are half-size. Indeed, there remains an ambivalence in Portugal about the period of Spanish rule, an ambivalence that was strongly seen from 1640 when the period ended. That ambivalence has not altered in recent years.

War in the Spanish System

Rule by the kings of Spain greatly compromised Portuguese imperial activity, security and expansion, and that was despite Portugal being linked to the strongest European empire. After 1580, Portuguese resources were, in large part, deliberately used to further Spanish interests in Europe and elsewhere. This process had its most dramatic form in 1588 when the Spanish Armada against England sailed from Lisbon while the brunt of the subsequent battles, notably that off Gravelines, was borne by Portuguese galleons with their heavy firepower. Philip had gone to war with England in 1585, a war that continued until 1604, while the conflict with Dutch rebels lasted from 1566 to 1609. Moreover, Philip intervened in France in a full-scale fashion from 1589 to 1598. Spain and its empire was put under great pressure from this combination of opponents and crises.

The Armada led to an English counter-blow in 1589, one designed to destroy the remnants of the Spanish fleet. At the same time, the presence of António offered the prospect of driving the Spaniards from Portugal and gaining commercial access to Lisbon. This aspiration was the motivation behind the substantial funding put up by merchants from the City of London. The result was the worst possible compromise. The force made a successful landing at Peniche on the Atlantic coast, some fifty miles from Lisbon. Hopes that the countryside would rise in support of António, however, proved totally unfounded. As the English troops trekked across the countryside towards Lisbon, losing men all the time to heat exhaustion and disease, Francis Drake, at the head of a squadron, sailed to the mouth of the Tagus, but he failed to force his way past the forts guarding the entrance to Lisbon.

Had the expedition sailed directly for Lisbon and seized the forts by an amphibious assault, as Alba had done in 1580, Lisbon would probably have fallen and, with it, the whole of Portugal. So also if Drake had forced his way past the forts and attacked Lisbon from its undefended waterfront. Indeed, in 1587, Drake had carried out extensive surveys of the estuary sending barques up to the port under cover of darkness. However, multiple aims and objectives, combined with a lack of vision or conviction on the part of Elizabeth I and of the commanders, squandered opportunities and nothing was achieved, unlike in 1596 when Cádiz was stormed by an Anglo-Dutch force. Even had Lisbon fallen, Philip II would have been able to mount a powerful counterattack.

The Cityscape

Lisbon was captured pictorially in 1598 in the fifth volume of *Civitates Orbis Terrarum*, a multi-volume atlas by Georg Braun, the editor, Georg Hoefnagel, an Antwerp-based Flemish painter, and other contributors. Dominating the skyline in the centre is the fortress of Castelo Sao Jorge, while the cathedral and the Ribeira Palace (which was to be destroyed in the earthquake) is prominent. The plan is accompanied by a key identifying 140 features. The Baixa is depicted with its original medieval street pattern. Rather like modern Portugal, there are windmills on a nearby hill.

The shift in the use of Portuguese resources to the service of Spain was of great importance because, prior to 1580, Portugal had enjoyed a significant window of opportunity. It had not been involved in the Italian Wars and the related Franco-Habsburg struggle for predominance of 1494–1559, nor in the 'Wars of Religion' stemming from the Reformation. Thus, unlike other European states, Portugal, with its narrow demographic base, had been able to devote its military resources to extra-European activity. It had thus achieved a military situation that prefigured the position of Britain for most of the century after victory at Waterloo in 1815; as an expansionist power on the edge of Europe and relatively disengaged from that continent's struggles.

In contrast, when Portugal became part of the Spanish system, it was targeted by attacks on that system, and became a tempting victim due to the wealth and apparent vulnerability of the Portuguese Empire. Prior to 1580, Portuguese global military–economic organisation had already faced many difficulties. These became much more acute after 1580. Whereas English attacks on Portuguese trade prior to 1580 had been small-scale and essentially on the Guinea coast, thereafter Portuguese possessions were directly affected by the upsurge in English attacks on the Spanish maritime and colonial world. East Indiamen, large carracks carrying enormous wealth, were attacked by English fleets as they sailed through the Azores en route to Portugal. In 1591, the *Madre de Deus* was captured and the *Santa Clara* destroyed by a fleet of English privateers off the Azores, although a third carrack, the *San Bernardo*, evaded another English force and arrived safely in Lisbon. After this, Portuguese ships avoided the Azores on their return journeys from the East.

The first English ship in the Indian Ocean arrived in 1591. The *Edward Bonaventure*, captained by James Lancaster, who had earlier served the Portuguese, captured three Portuguese ships in 1592. Lancaster went on to command a fleet that captured the Portuguese base of Pernambuco in Brazil with great booty in 1595, and to command the first fleet of the English East India Company formed in 1600.

The Dutch also became a serious threat. Philip banned Dutch trade with Lisbon in 1594, encouraging the Dutch to seek spices at their Asian sources. In 1596, the first Dutch fleet reached Bantam in West Java and, in 1602, the Dutch first landed on Sri Lanka, challenging the Portuguese position there. In 1605, local rulers received Dutch help in driving the Portuguese from

Ambon, Ternate and Tidore in the Spice Islands. Moreover, the Portuguese now lacked the diplomatic independence necessary in order to consider how best to respond to such attacks.

The threat of attacks on the coast, which included the English sacking of Faro in 1596, led Philip to order defence precautions, such as the fortifications begun in 1592 to protect the port of Viana do Castelo. The ramparts can be visited there. In addition, the citadel built at Setúbal in 1595 was designed to protect and control the Sado estuary.

The Growth of a Slave-Sugar Economy

The period of Spanish rule saw a major growth in a slave-sugar economy based in Brazil. Slavery was longstanding in Portugal, being found under the Romans and Moors. Thus, raids on Lisbon (1189) and Silves (1191) each yielded the Moors about 3000 slaves. In turn, after the *Reconquista*, enslaved Muslims helping provide workers, notably agricultural labour in the south. Expeditions along the coast of West Africa were motivated by a search for gold, but securing slaves soon became significant. The Portuguese found it difficult to gain entry into the gold trade from the interior of West Africa, but they did so, in part because slaves became useful as a commodity to sell in exchange for gold, rather as the British were later to use Indian opium in China. Moreover, and more significantly, alongside the use of slaves for trade in Africa, the Portuguese also exploited them as a labour force in Portugal and on the developing sugar plantations of Madeira. Between 140,000 and 170,000 slaves were exported to Portugal or Madeira from 1441 to 1505. In Portugal, most worked in domestic service. By the mid-sixteenth century, about a tenth of the population of Lisbon and the Algarve were slaves, although the percentage in Oporto was only about five. Lagos in the Algarve became a slave market. Slaves were brought in during the fifteenth century, and indeed up to the nineteenth century, to cultivate rice and work the salt fields in the Algarve and the Sado Valley. They built on the use of Muslims as workers and compensated for the movement of Portuguese overseas. Genetic studies have revealed high sub-Saharan maternal lineages, one of 2010 in Alcácer producing a figure of 22 per cent, the highest in Europe.

The sub-Saharan source of slaves encouraged the Italian commercial and financial interests that had been significant for the trade in slaves from the Black Sea, which was cut by the Turkish advance, to transfer their expertise and capital instead to the new Portuguese-controlled African slave trade. Like the Black Sea trade, the new one involved permanent overseas protected bases for trade, long-range shipment by sea, and the ability to invest capital for returns that were not going to be made for a while. The role of Italian intermediaries was shown when, in 1470, Bartolomeo Marchionni, the agent for a Florentine family involved in the Black Sea slave trade, moved to Lisbon, from where he developed sugar plantations in Madeira and gained from the Crown a privileged position in the slave trade on the Guinea coast.

Physical prowess was a key element in the assessment of slaves by the Portuguese. This criterion was important because the spread of sugar cultivation, an arduous task, became a leading prompt to the slave trade. This was thanks to the establishment of plantation slavery on Madeira, which, in the fifteenth century, became the leading producer of sugar in the Portuguese world.

This provided a pattern for Brazil. The alternatives were limited. The enslavement of the native population was a crucial source of labour, but the natives either fled before the raiders or resisted them. Moreover, some of the areas in the Brazilian interior into which raids were conducted were distant from the coastal centres of agriculture. As a result, native slaves were most important in frontier regions, notably Amazonia, that were distant from the coastal points of arrival of African slaves. Failure in Morocco meant that raising slaves from the Moors was no longer an option as it had been in the fifteenth century. Portuguese peasants were moved to Brazil, but this proved a limited resource, and one not suited for the arduous labour regime in the sugar plantations. In contrast, moving peasants to the Azores and Madeira, where tasks were less arduous, was more successful.

Brazil rapidly became the leading producer of sugar in the Portuguese world, enjoying as it did a major advantage due to slave labour, as well as a lengthy harvest season, comparatively mild weather and relatively fresh (uncultivated) soil in plentiful quantities. Indeed, the seizure of lands with fresh soil was crucial to Western expansion in the Americas. The number of sugar mills in Brazil rose from 60 in 1570 to 192 in around 1600. The initial emphasis was on native labour, but this was hit hard by a smallpox epidemic in 1560–3 and by a measles epidemic in 1563. As a result of a shortage of labour, the Portuguese turned to importing slaves from West Africa and Angola. The north-east coast of Brazil, the centre of sugar production, and its ports, such as Recife and Bahia, were close to Africa, which underlined the capacity of oceans to link rather than divide. This was a key aspect of the Portuguese world. Relatively short slave voyages were particularly valuable because they reduced the need for credit in bridging the period between the purchase and sale of slaves, while death rates among the slaves were generally lower on shorter voyages.

By the mid-1580s, about one-third of the slaves in Brazil were Africans, and by 1620, as a result of the growth in the slave trade, they were in a majority. In the last quarter of the sixteenth century, about 40,000 African slaves entered Brazil in a trade that provided revenues to the Crown as, aside from slaves moved on the royal account, private slave traders were taxed. Developing at a major rate from the 1570s, sugar production helped ensure that Brazil alone received 42 per cent of the slaves imported into the Americas during the seventeenth century. Indeed, the number who arrived in Brazil exceeded that of the white settlers. This flow was necessary because, on the sugar estates in Brazil, slaves had a life expectancy of fewer than eight years. The profits of slavery encouraged the further expansion of Portuguese Brazil, and notably so along its northern coast, where the captaincies of Ceará, Maranhão and Pará were founded in 1613, 1615 and 1616 respectively, and new settlements included Belém do Pará in 1616. As with São Paulo, this was settlement to the west of the demarcation line under the Treaty of Tordesillas.

The 'white gold' sugar economy of Brazil brought Portugal great wealth, but also made it a target. After the expiry of a twelve-year truce agreed in 1609, war between the Dutch and Spanish resumed in 1621. Portugal was therefore a target. The Dutch focused on north-east Brazil, where they captured Recife in 1630. This effort and success reflected the relative value and vulnerability of the Portuguese colonies.

The disruption to sugar production in Brazil due to the war led to a marked shift in production to the West Indies. This was part of a wider crisis in the Portuguese Empire. Thus, in 1637, the Dutch captured São Jorge da Mina, which they renamed Elmina. The Portuguese never won it back. Also in West Africa, Shama (Fort São Sebastião) was lost to the Dutch in 1637, Axim in 1642 and Accra in 1659. None were regained. Indeed, the contest in West Africa became that between the English and the Dutch.

The Dutch also attacked the Portuguese positions in Asia, although they failed at Macao in 1622. The attack by the Dutch was an aspect of a more general pressure on the Portuguese Empire. In 1629, Malacca survived a major assault by Sultan Iskandar Muda of Aceh, in large part thanks to help from the Sultan of Johor, but Hormuz fell to attack by Abbas I of Persia in 1622. It had lacked adequate artillery. Moreover, hostile English action ensured that Hormuz lacked naval support. In Sri Lanka, the Portuguese were put under great pressure from the inland kingdom of Kandy. In 1630, at Randeniwela, the Portuguese army on the island was ambushed and the Captain-General killed. In

1638, there was another defeat and the death of another Captain-General. In 1640, joint attacks by the Dutch and the Kandyans led to the fall of the Portuguese-held Galle and Negombo.

The End of Union

The strains of these conflicts put pressure on the links between Portugal and Spain. So also did the heavy financial demands of the latter as it faced sustained conflict in the 1620s and 1630s against France as well as the Dutch and German princes. These demands placed a strain on assumptions about fair kingship. These assumptions were also under even greater pressure due to the economic depression that affected most of seventeenth-century Europe. Agricultural productivity declined, while taxation demands and those for troops fell on a stagnant economy. Indeed, in 1628, a tax on linen led to rioting by women in Oporto.

Hostility to Spain became more apparent. Philip III of Spain (r. 1598–1621), Philip II of Portugal, had neglected Portugal, only visiting it in 1619 in order to have the *cortes* affirm the succession of his son, and doing so with the protection of Spanish troops. He favoured Spaniards for posts there. Moreover, in Portugal as elsewhere, Philip IV of Spain (r. 1621–65), Philip III of Portugal, proved less adroit than his grandfather, and his focus on appointing Spaniards in Portugal was highly unwelcome. He also broke the guarantees made by Philip I of Portugal. An awareness of the problems posed by Spanish rule was driven home by Dutch attacks on the Portuguese Empire.

Other states were also in serious difficulties, notably Britain where rebellion in Scotland started in 1638. In the Spanish world, rebellion began in Catalonia in May 1640. As a result, the troops in Iberia were focused on trying to suppress the rebellion there. This provided an opportunity for rebellion in Portugal, while the demand that Portuguese nobles join the forces preparing to act against Catalonia forced them to make a choice. There had been rioting in 1637 across southern Portugal, beginning in Évora with opposition to new taxes.

There was a full-scale rebellion on 1 December 1640 on behalf of Portuguese independence, which was expressed in terms of the claims of one of Portugal's leading nobles, the hesitant John, 8th Duke of Braganza. John had claims on the throne through his grandmother Catherine, a granddaughter of Manuel I, whose claim had been mentioned in 1580, and through his great-great grandfather, a nephew of Manuel. The key element was that of opportunity. An unpopular, vulnerable Spanish administration proved unable to resist. In the coup that was staged by the Forty Conspirators and their supporters, Miguel de Vasconcelos, the Secretary of State from 1635, and one of his juniors, were murdered, and Margaret of Savoy, the Viceroy from 1635, a cousin of Philip III of Portugal and a descendant of Manuel I, was allowed to leave for Spain. She had been sent to Lisbon because she out-ranked John, whom the Spaniards had tried to get out of the way by appointing him to posts in their empire, only to meet with his refusal. The somewhat politically quiescent John, a musician of talent, had refused to back the rioting in 1637, and he was not at the forefront of the 1640 conspiracy. His being summoned to Madrid brought it forward. The key backers of the rebellion were lesser nobles, the lower clergy, the Jesuits and the Archbishop of Lisbon. French agents encouraged the discontent.

Margaret was made to sign orders to the Spanish garrisons to surrender their positions, and all did, bar Ceuta and Angra in the Azores. John was declared John IV of Portugal on 7 December 1640. The result was war, a conflict that lasted until 1668. This restoration of independence is commemorated in central Lisbon with the obelisk erected in 1886 in the *Praça dos Restauradores*. The obelisk records the names and dates of the battles in the War of Restoration, while the bronze figures on the pedestal show Victory and Freedom.

7. Baroque Portugal, 1640–1750

The focus in the long war with Spain from 1640 to 1668 was on frontier conflict and the search for international support, because within Portugal the new regime rapidly consolidated its position. In October 1641, a counter-revolution on behalf of Spain, attributed to the Inquisition, was quelled, and those involved were executed or, as with the Archbishop of Braga, Sebastião de Matos de Noronha (a Spaniard), and the Inquisitor General, Francisco de Castro, imprisoned for life. No new Inquisitor was appointed until 1671.

So also with officials regarded as unreliable, such as Francisco de Lucena, the new Secretary of State or head of government, who was removed in 1642 and executed in 1643 for alleged links with Spain; although, in part, this execution reflected pressure on John IV from the *cortes*. As part of the morbid character of politics, Lucena was beheaded with the same cleaver used in earlier executions against those charged with treason. Many of the greater nobility were opposed to the new regime.

Opposition to Spain brought alliances with the Dutch, France and Sweden in 1641, and with England in 1642, but not the marriage alliance, and therefore dynastic recognition, with France that was sought. Moreover, the war with the Dutch in the colonies continued and, as a result, Portugal as well as the Portuguese world were still under great pressure.

The war with Spain, Portugal's longest war in modern times, helped define the following period of Portuguese history in domestic and international terms, and in political and cultural ways, to a degree that is difficult to appreciate today. In the war, the nature of the campaigning zone encouraged a resort to cavalry. This was not least because of the difficulty of mounting operations with large infantry forces in what, due in part to the hot climate, were short campaigning seasons, in which such forces moved slowly, which increased the burden of feeding them. The use of cavalry was also favoured by a tactical emphasis on irregular warfare with, in particular, the ambush of crucial supply convoys. Raids, moreover, led to scorched-earth tactics in order to make defensive positions untenable, as well as providing a display of power that was particularly important in seeking to maintain support and sow fear.

Bridging points were crucial, reflecting the limited number of bridges. The nature of supply links meant that these points were key nexuses for road systems reliant on crossing rivers. Moreover, rivers offered both obstacles and significant defensive positions. New or improved fortifications, such as the Fort of St Francis finished in Chaves in 1658, the two fortresses in Valença do Minho, and the defences of Almeida and Sabugal, enhanced Portugal's defences.

Frontier conflict became acute in 1644 with the Portuguese victorious at Montijo and the city of Elvas successfully resisting a Spanish siege. (Elvas's fortifications are now a UNESCO World Heritage site that can be viewed from a walk around the top of the walls.) In the 1640s and 1650s, however, Spain, rather than concentrating on Portugal, focused on war with France and on the eventually successful suppression of the rebellion in Catalonia, which was finally achieved in 1652. This focus reflected the threat posed by France's intervention in Catalonia. Furthermore, in 1654, Portugal signed a treaty with England, then ruled by Oliver Cromwell and opposed to Spain. This both brought help and lessened the number of enemies. Elvas was besieged again in 1659, only for the Spaniards to be routed on 17 January by a relief force that had advanced in a dense mist.

The Peace of the Pyrenees between France and Spain in 1659 enabled Spain, instead, to focus on Portugal, a process aided by peace with England soon after. Furthermore, the Treaty of The Hague with the Dutch in 1661 had the same effect for Portugal. Faced by the new challenge, the Portuguese raised international forces, notably in England and Scotland where mercenaries, spare after the end of the British civil wars and the Thirty Years War, were hired. Charles II married the Portuguese King's sister, Catherine of Braganza, in 1662, and she provided Tangier and Bombay as her dowry. Portugal also benefited from continued French help despite the French promise to Spain in 1659 to stop providing assistance.

With Philip IV (r. 1621–65) determined not to accept the loss of Portugal and still seeing himself as Philip III of Portugal, Spain repeatedly attacked, but unsuccessfully so. In 1663, the Spaniards, who had overrun southern Portugal and captured Évora on 22 May, were heavily defeated at Ameixial, north-west of Estremoz, en route to Lisbon. Fought on 8 June, this was a key victory, with heavy Spanish casualties – about 8000 to 10,000 killed or wounded compared to 1000 Portuguese – and all the Spanish cannon captured. In the battle:

The English [helping the Portuguese] marched on shouting as if victorious, but discharged no shot till they came within push of pike of the enemy, and then they poured in their shot so thick upon them that made them quit their ground and fly towards the left wing, leaving their cannon behind them, which afterwards turned upon them, much to their prejudice. Notwithstanding the rich baggages and coaches and wealthy plunder which were on top of the hill – the English seeing the field not cleared – there was not one man of them stirred out of his rank, but kept close serried together to prevent any second onset, which immediately followed for they were assaulted front, flank and rear by divers of the enemy's troops of horse, but having their fire ready at all hands, they quickly quitted themselves of those troops. This was performed rather with an absolute resolution than any conduct or order, for after the soldiers had serried themselves close no officer's voice could be heard, but each soldier would give the word of command either as they saw or feared their enemy, but all this while a man could not but joy to see so vivid a courage and so firm a resolution as was in every common soldier to die by one another.

There were 3000 British auxiliaries in the Portuguese army, while the larger Spanish one included Italian and German troops. The Portuguese commander was Sancho Manoel de Vilhena, 1st Count of Vila Flor, who had earlier fought the Dutch in Brazil and at Elvas in 1659.

Later that month, the Spanish garrison in Évora surrendered. In 1664, there was another impressive Portuguese military performance at Castelo Rodrigo, again in the face of a larger Spanish force. A marker, erected in 1940, commemorates the success.

Lastly, at Montes Claros near Vila Viçosa on 17 June 1665, yet another larger Spanish force was defeated. The Spaniards had planned to march on Lisbon, but were delayed by the siege of Vila Viçosa, and this hit the dynamism of the Spanish advance as well as the numbers in their force. The fighting quality and persistence of the Portuguese saw off a series of Spanish attacks, and, after seven hours, a Portuguese counterattack routed the Spaniards who lost many men and all the artillery. The English infantry on the Portuguese side faced the Swiss infantry under Spanish service, well-known for their reputation in close combat since the fifteenth century. The English employed their usual tactic of approaching close to the enemy, firing a few volleys, and then charging with pikes and muskets used as clubs. At Montes Claros, unlike at Ameixial, the enemy infantry did not run away and, therefore, a fierce, close combat ensued. According to a contemporary account, the fighting between the two opposing infantry lines raged around a stone well:

> And the two commanders Ingaging [*sic*] one another with their Pikes, the Switzer had the Honour to kill Mr. Shelton, Lieutenant-Colonel to Count *Schombergs* Regiment of Infantry; upon which Major *Maire* generously, to revenge the Death of his Commandant, attacking likewise the Switzer with his Pike, and overthrowing him with such a Blow as the other had giv'n Lieutenant Colonel Shelton, made them equal in their Fate as in their Courage.

The Portuguese were commanded by António Luís de Meneses, Count of Cantanhede, who had played a key role in the 1640 coup and in the battle at Elvas in 1659. In 1661, he was made Marquis of Marialva.

This was the last attempted invasion in that war. The ministers of Philip's physically and mentally weak successor, the infant Charles II (r. 1665–1700), were not in a position to persist in the struggle. Indeed, Spain declared bankruptcy again in 1666. The conflict, however, continued until the Treaty of Lisbon of 13 February 1668, a treaty mediated by Edward, 1st Earl of Sandwich, brought Spanish recognition of Portuguese independence and of the sovereignty of the house of Braganza. Spain was now more worried about French pressure, notably in the Low Countries in the War of Devolution, which the French had launched with great success in 1667.

One legacy of the war of independence is the Battle Room in the Palace of the Marquês de Fronteira, which was built in 1671. The title of Marquês de Fronteira was granted to Dom João de Mascarenhas, 2nd Count of Torre, to reward his participation in the war. The Italianate garden is also impressive. Another legacy is the impressive fort on Berlenga Grande, an island nature reserve off Peniche.

John IV had died in 1656, leaving as his successor Afonso VI, a minor and, more seriously, the victim of illness, probably meningitis. He appeared both unfit and uncontrollable, a marked contrast to Louis XIV. Afonso survived a coup in 1662, but his marriage to Marie Françoise (Maria Francisca) of Savoy-Nemours (1646–83) in 1666 proved a disaster. She formed a relationship with Afonso's brother, Peter, Duke of Beja, who persuaded Afonso to abdicate, a situation recognised by the *cortes* in 1668. Peter became, first, regent and then Peter II.

World War

Victory over Spain did not mean victory in Portugal's mid-century world war. This had been a war with the Dutch, as Spain was unable to attack Portugal's colonies. Indeed, only Ceuta was lost to Spain, and that because it did not join the Braganza revolution in 1640. It remains Spanish to this day, although there are signs of the over two centuries of Portuguese rule, including wall tiles. Had Ceuta continued Portuguese, it would probably have been eventually ceded to Morocco.

The Dutch had been engaged in full-scale conflict with the Portuguese prior to the 1640 rebellion, and the subsequent rebellion did not change this. Brazil was a key area for conflict. Already, in the 1630s, the Dutch dynamic of success had declined as the Neapolitan troops in Portuguese/Spanish service proved better able than their Dutch opponents to adapt to the possibilities of the terrain, adopting far more open formations as well as using frequent ambushes. In the 1640s, the balance moved in favour of the Portuguese, with a widespread rebellion by Portuguese planters in 1645 against Dutch rule. A major Dutch expedition sent in 1647 failed to stabilise the situation by capturing Bahia.

The strain of war on the Portuguese economy was shown by the foundation in 1649 of *Companhia Geral do Comércio do Brasil* (General Company for Trade of Brazil). It was founded with considerable monopolies and other trading advantages, in return for an agreement to provide thirty-six warships to convoy merchantmen to Brazil, a formidable, but necessary, protection against Dutch attack. However, a series of difficulties, including a lack of finance, led to its incorporation into the Crown in 1664. Convoys thereafter were provided on a reduced scale.

The Dutch position in Brazil had also been weakened by a lack of support for all-out war with Portugal from within the United Provinces, and from the need for the Dutch to focus on war with England in 1652–4. In 1654, Recife and the other Dutch positions surrendered to the Portuguese, although the Treaty of Taborda was only a truce. Recife was important because the value of a colony derived in large part from its ability to trade.

The Dutch were more successful in Asia where, in alliance with the inland kingdom of Kandy, they drove the Portuguese from coastal Sri Lanka in 1638–42 after a conflict in which the Portuguese made a major effort. The Dutch also seized Malacca (1641), benefiting, unlike in 1629, from the help of Johore, and the Portuguese bases on the Malabar coast of India. These losses were not regained.

Also in 1641, the Dutch captured the island of Fernando Pó, and the ports of Luanda and Benguela in Angola. Kongo, an ally from earlier in the century, provided the Dutch with support. However, these positions were recaptured in 1648, with the Portuguese using a fleet from Brazil. These recaptures, a reminder of the interconnected sides of the Atlantic, provided the basis for a marked revival of the integrated Portuguese slave and sugar economy in the South Atlantic. The latter indeed became a key unit in the Portuguese world. The Treaty of The Hague of 1661 saw the Dutch recognise Brazil as Portuguese in return for four million *réis* over sixteen years.

The Portuguese were also under pressure from other powers. In a longstanding pattern, the fate of Portuguese positions often reflected not so much their inherent strength or weakness, but rather the possibility of relief and recapture, and the interaction of local rivalries with broader patterns of great-power antagonism. The prospect or not of relief was a crucial factor. Although Goa successfully resisted attacks by the sultanate of Bijapur in 1654 and 1659, and by the Marathas in 1683, the positions on the Kanara coast of India fell in the 1650s. Furthermore, the Omani Arabs, having captured Muscat in 1650, developed a navy and attacked Portuguese positions around the Arabian Sea, sacking Diu in 1668 and 1676, and raiding Mozambique in 1670, culminating with the capture of Mombasa in 1698 after a long siege of Fort Jesus. The siege began in 1696, when the garrison consisted of only fifty Portuguese soldiers and a force of loyal coast Arabs. However, it was strengthened by relief forces brought by sea in 1696 and 1697. The garrison was able to see off the impact of the weak cannon of the besiegers, but succumbed to disease, notably beriberi, and hunger. The Omanis fired corpses into the fort, contributing to the spread of an epidemic.

A sense of crisis in the Portuguese Empire was also seen in the disastrous defeat, at Kitombo in 1670, of the attempt to intervene in the Kongolese civil war. Moreover, Portuguese expansion in Angola stalled in the 1680s and in the Zambezi Valley in the early 1690s. As in the sixteenth century, the effectiveness of Portuguese musketeers was reduced by their slow rate of fire and by the non-linear, open-order fighting methods of their opponents. Moreover, supply problems and disease hit the Portuguese hard.

Peter II, 1668–1706

The international situation put Portugal under serious pressure. This was accentuated by the extent to which its dynastic, ministerial and aristocratic politics were linked to international tensions, with powerful French and Spanish parties within Portugal at court, among the greater aristocracy and in the Church hierarchy. Peter II had to take careful note of the domestic situation. From 1668, he was regent for Afonso VI whom he kept in the Azores and later in Sintra until Afonso died in 1683, whereupon Peter became king, ruling until 1706. In 1668, Peter also married Afonso's wife, Marie Françoise (Maria Francisca) of Savoy; as her first marriage was never consummated, she obtained an annulment. The vexed politics of these years involved the Inquisition. Indeed, in response to a report by António Vieira, one of its victims, and to a judicial investigation, Pope Innocent XI suspended it in Portugal from 1674 to 1681.

Signing the Treaty of Lisbon with Spain in 1668 was a major gain, and enabled Peter to focus on an 'absolutist' agenda similar to that of other European monarchies. In response to the mid-century crisis when the nobility had gained power at the expense of the royal government, Peter moved the focus back to the latter. On the pattern of France, he also followed a mercantilist policy of trying to develop trade and industry, notably textiles.

Peter, however, was placed under strong pressure to take sides in European warfare, notably, prior to 1700, to align with France or its then leading opponent, Spain. Louis XIV's standing as godfather to his daughter in 1669 symbolised the paternal and protective nature of the alliance between the two powers. In a society where claims to property at every level of society were defended tenaciously, and renunciations of rights in treaties subsequently denied, there was no reason to believe that Spain would relax her interest in regaining Portugal.

The alliance with France was not, however, one that was unduly subservient on Portugal's part. In 1669, pressure to support proposed French action in the East Indies against the Dutch was resisted. In 1672, Portugal did not join Louis XIV of France and Charles II of England in their attack on the Dutch.

In 1675, Louis's attempt to incite Portugal to join him in his war against Spain failed, a marked contrast with his success in bringing Sweden into the war against Prussia. Peter had good reasons. In 1659, France had abandoned Portugal when negotiating with Spain and there was a danger that such a desertion would be repeated. Furthermore, France's principal interest in any war with Spain, the Spanish Netherlands (modern Belgium), was not central to Spain's concern. In any Franco-Portuguese war with Spain, France might conquer the Spanish Netherlands, and Spain, instead, attack the more vulnerable Portugal rather than France. Portugal's problem as an ally of France was similar to that of many second-rank states: unable to gain advantages without powerful allies, but all too easy to drop in the kaleidoscopic nature of alliance politics.

Similarly, Portugal posed for France the problem that minor allies posed for major states. Such allies tended to offer support only when they required assistance, their demands (as Britain was to discover in the case of Portugal in 1735 and 1762) were usually heavy and inconvenient, and, when, in contrast, their aid was needed by the major power, it was often refused.

Religion could be a factor in the debate over choices. In early 1689, court preachers told Peter to attack the Dutch, France's enemy, in the Indian Ocean in order to retake earlier losses to the Protestants. At the same time, the Dutch envoy was citing the support William III of Orange, who had recently seized Britain from its Catholic ruler, received from Catholic Austria and Bavaria against France as proof that his policy was not a confessional one. Peter, 'the Pacific', did nothing. In 1699, when casting about for an acceptable choice, who had to be Catholic, William III suggested Peter as a candidate for the succession to the childless Charles II of Spain, but Louis XIV of France rejected him.

Not taking part in the Dutch (1672–8) or Nine Years (1688–97) wars, Portugal avoided war with other European powers between 1668 and 1703, an unusual feat for Portugal in recent decades, although one seen prior to 1580. This neutrality required care outside Europe as well as within. Thus, in 1697–1700, there was a dispute over Maranhão, in Brazil north of the Amazon, with France pressing for an Amazon frontier for its colony of Cayenne, a frontier that would have included part of northern Brazil. However, conflict was avoided and, ultimately, Louis did not press the issue as he wanted to win Portugal's backing in Europe.

As Europe moved toward war over the Spanish succession, Peter backed France. Louis's second grandson, Philip, Duke of Anjou, became Philip V of Spain in 1700, which brought Bourbon power to Portugal's frontiers. Peter changed sides in May 1703 only as a result of successful Anglo-Dutch naval action at Vigo nearby in Spain in 1702, the threat of Anglo-Dutch naval attack on Lisbon, the prospect of territorial gains for Portugal, and the promise of the candidature of an Austrian prince for the Spanish throne. This was a guarantee of support from the Allies (Austria, Britain and the Dutch) and offered a less threatening neighbour than a Bourbon. In contrast, Louis XIV made it clear that he would not be able to provide the degree of naval protection the Portuguese requested. Peter certainly feared Anglo-Dutch naval attack, which was no idle fear in light of the exposed nature of Portuguese maritime routes and the Portuguese coast. This factor was accentuated by the significance of Brazilian gold and the terrible state of Portugal's navy. The same year, Victor Amadeus II of Savoy-Piedmont also changed sides, leaving his French alliance for one with Austria, England and the Dutch. The second-rank powers had to manoeuvre with care.

The Facts of Life

In the background to politics, much of life remained grim as, indeed, for most Portuguese was the case until the second half of the twentieth century. The situation was common to Europe as a whole, indeed to much of the world, rather than specifically Portugal; but that should not mean that it should be excluded from a book on Portugal because it was important to an understanding of life there in the past. Aside from epidemics, such as plague in 1505, sanitation and diet were major problems for the bulk of the population. Their housing conditions, in particular the habit of sharing beds, were conducive to a high incidence of respiratory infections. This was a consequence of the lack of privacy that was produced by the limited nature of the housing stock.

Louse infestation was related to crowding, inadequate bathing facilities and the continual wearing of the same clothes. Cleanliness was associated with wearing clean shirts and linen, rather than washing, but both were only possible for a minority. Whatever their wealth, humans had few defences against a whole range of the natural world, from lice, bedbugs and fleas to tapeworms.

The habit of washing in clean water was perforce limited, while the proximity to humans of animals and dunghills was unhelpful. Like the rest of Europe, Portugal was a society that conserved, rather than disposed of, its excrement. Animal and human waste were gathered for the purpose of manure, a crucial replenishment of soil fertility, and necessarily so in the absence of the guano imports of the nineteenth century and the synthesised fertilisers of more recent times.

However, this manure was a health hazard, notably through contaminating the water supply. Effluent from undrained privies and animal pens flowed across streets, and on and beneath the surface, into houses through generally porous walls. Typhus was one result. Although the risk of disease is now far less, the old parts of many Portuguese settlements still tend to smell of 'drains' or, rather, their absence or inadequacy. Another legacy of the search for fertiliser can still be seen across Portugal, with pigeon- and dovecotes providing fertiliser and eventually, when the pigeons were old or when hunger necessitated, food. So also with the gathering of seaweed for fertiliser, notably in the large lagoon near Aveiro, a practice that continues today.

Alongside the availability, in towns from Roman times, of public fountains and public taps in streets, clean drinking water was an issue across much of Portugal, especially in coastal regions and lowland areas without deep wells. River water was often muddy and could be contaminated by animal and human excrement, while pump water could be affected by sewage. As elsewhere in Europe, this situation accounted for the importance of fermented drinks.

Reminding us anew that a history of Portugal is in part a history of Europe, poor nutrition also contributed to the spread of infectious diseases by lowering resistance. Furthermore, malnutrition limited sexual desire and activity, hindered successful pregnancy, and, if chronic, delayed sexual maturity and produced sterility in women. Malnutrition was not the sole issue: unsuccessful pregnancies repeatedly proved a problem for the royal family. Problems of food shortage and cost ensured that the bulk of the population lacked a balanced diet, even when they had enough food. Diet was a particular problem for the urban poor, who found fruit and vegetables, let alone meat and fish, expensive, and who were also frequently ill clad. Although the range of crops had been expanded with the exploration of the New World, from which maize was introduced, the peasantry consumed little meat or fish.

This pattern looks toward the nature of modern Portuguese cuisine, and notably so with it being low on beef. Bread-based meals remain important, as do non-meat soups, such as *Sopa de Castanhas piladas* from Trás-os-Montes, a soup with beans, dried chestnuts and rice.

Hunting was a key source of meat as well as a means of recreation for the socially prominent. Recipes for rabbit, such as the Alentejan dish *coelho em vinho*, reflect this to this day. Tile panels, originally in the palace of the Viscount of Valmor in Lisbon, now displayed in the museum at Lamego, show birds and deer being shot. Fishing is depicted in the hypnotically soothing tile panels in the cloisters of Oporto cathedral.

Disease was not only affected by nutrition. Harsh weather, notably, but not only, in the winter, could weaken resistance. It was exacerbated by shortages of firewood and by the damp, cold, cramped, crowded and insanitary nature of much accommodation. The persistence of disease ensured that weaker members of the community remained especially vulnerable. The real killer of babies was puerperal fever, the cause of which was not understood until the nineteenth century. Even royal children could have a poor rate of survival.

Politico-social factors, however, were also significant in famine and disease. Subsistence crises were not simply the result of demand exceeding the amount of food available, important as that was, but also had their roots in the markedly unequal distribution of resources in Portugal and in the limitations of governmental action, however much the latter was alleviated by religious charity, both the work of religious foundations and lay almsgiving. This is a pattern that has continued to the present.

The situation at the level of the individual was of a hostile and unpredictable environment, of forces that could be neither prevented nor propitiated, and of the efforts of years swept away in an instant. The line between independence and calamity, between being poor and falling into pauperdom, could be crossed easily, fast and frequently. Until about 1750, Portuguese GDP per capita was reasonably high when compared to other Western European countries, but that was scarcely a condition of ease, and after that high point there was a massive depression in the economy and in living standards, from which Portugal only recovered in the twentieth century, more particularly in the last quarter.

Pension provisions in Baroque Portugal were non-existent for the bulk of the population, and the latter, therefore, had to work until they dropped. Ill health was regarded with great foreboding. Bleeding was the cure recommended by Portuguese doctors for most conditions. Vaccination arrived late, while doctors were socially despised and their reputation was also affected by the fact that some were 'New Christians' or suspected of being so. Reform came largely through foreign doctors.

The art of the period includes that on the wonderful *azulejos* (tiles) that can be seen in situ, as well as in Lisbon's superb tile museum, which is housed in the attractive church and cloisters of a former monastery (the restaurant can be recommended). This art, however, did not capture the grim working conditions of the age. For example, fishing was extremely dangerous, with the small boats subject to storms and tides, a situation that has lasted to the present, although engines have transformed the situation. Moreover, many places of craft work and industrial employment, including those involved in the production of works of art, craft and architecture, were damp, poorly ventilated, badly lit or dangerous. Exposure to hazardous substances, such as lead and mercury, was a serious problem, while construction work was highly dangerous. Millers worked in dusty and noisy circumstances, frequently suffered from lice and often developed asthma, hernias and chronic back problems. The notions of health and safety at work were barely understood, and the issues involved were generally not grasped.

Agriculture was highly vulnerable to the weather and to disease, and to a far greater extent than in the modern age. There were few improved crop strains, and rainy autumns produced diseased and swollen crops, while late frosts attacked wheat and other crops. Summer drought and winter cold were serious issues. The vintage was particularly susceptible to the weather and to disease. The absence of pesticides, and the difficulties in protecting crops and stored foods, were serious issues. Mice and rats posed major problems for food storage. The absence of refrigeration forced a reliance on smoking and salting, both of which have greatly affected the modern Portuguese diet. Spices helped to disguise the taste of smoking and salting, as did cooking in wine.

Animal health, moreover, was a serious issue. The primitive nature of veterinary science was a problem, and the usual response was the slaughter of animals and the prohibition of their movement. The facts of life were frequently deadly, for both humans and animals.

Transport links were poor. Bad roads ensured that the 300-km journey between Lisbon and Oporto took about a week. The lack of regulating dams ensured that floods did much damage, for example in Oporto. In Amarante, a flood destroyed the bridge in 1763. The state of the roads and the limited number of navigable rivers protected local industry from imports, including competition from elsewhere in Portugal. Self-production within the household, the village and the wider community was crucial to feeding and supplying the people. This process very much affected the roles of men and women.

Linked to the role of local production, it is necessary to note the diversity of Portuguese life, an element that continues today, albeit lessened by modern transport, education, communications and shopping. People adapted to the possibilities of the environment, as with the terracing of slopes for farming, with the major patterns of transhumance (animals moving to and from upland summer grazing) across much of Portugal, and with those who gathered annually to fish tuna. Transhumance is still practised in the Peneda-Gerês national park in the north. Another aspect of adaptation in that area is the *espigueiros* near Soajo. These granite caskets built on stilts to store harvested corn cobs above the wet soil also testified to popular piety as there were crosses on top.

Society

There was, in practice, much continuity, both during the seventeenth century and with the centuries on either side, and in some respects, albeit often below the surface, to the present. Society was very much stratified, with the weight of the past particularly present in status and privilege, but also in property, notably landed property, marital links and power. Social control by the élite was a fact, not an issue, in politics. Heredity and stability were regarded as intertwined, and snobbery was inherent, and clearly so in concern with rank, status and lineage. Society was truly divided. The rate of social change was rigidly governed by a variety of devices, including marital strategies, inheritance practices and government patronage. Each plays a continuing role today, although not to the same extent or with the same impact.

Women were very much under control, and were certainly more confined than in Britain. In Lisbon, the visiting Thomas Pelham got great pleasure from his visit to the splendid opera in 1775, adding: 'the orchestra is remarkable good and most of the singers; the scenery and dresses very expensive and rich but the dancing is very indifferent . . . there is one extraordinary circumstance in this opera that no ladies are admitted nor any women suffered to appear on the stage.' This was a product of the views of the Queen, of Catholic teaching and, even more, of the conservative observance of it in Portugal, a society that was more conservative than France.

There were tensions within society, a society structured by division; but it would be misleading to suggest either that there was widespread criticism of the existence of a hereditary hierarchical society, or that tensions were only apparent between, as distinct from within, social groups. The peasantry and the nobility, far from being uniform, were generally legally defined groups characterised by internal differences. Nobles vied with one another for local political power and social eminence, a process matched by that of peasants within their own communities.

Power and wealth within Portugal were concentrated in the hands of a relatively small number of families, whose coats of arms publicly and frequently displayed their importance, and in life as well as death. The ostentatiously hierarchical nature, both of society and of the dominant political system; the predominantly agrarian nature of the economy; the generally slow rate of change in social and economic affairs or, at least, of structural change; the unwillingness of monarchs, and of the noble-dominated government, to challenge fundamentally the interests of the nobility, or to govern without its cooperation; and the inegalitarian assumptions of the period: all combined to ensure that the concentration of power and wealth remained reasonably constant. Individual monarchs, such as John II, clashed with the greater nobility, but that was more a matter of resisting direction by individual nobles as any attempt to remould the sociology of power.

There was considerable social stability, not least because most wealth was inherited or acquired by marriage. Entails to maintain estates intact were available. Most land lost by individual noble families was not lost from the nobility, but, instead, generally, by marriage or sale, so as to be transferred to other nobles or to those who were ennobled. These factors were generally true in Europe.

As with other countries, most Portuguese nobles were poor, and many were similar to English gentry. The nobles lacked power and wealth, although, in comparison with the bulk of the population, they could be fairly placed in those categories. With the exception of the greater aristocracy, most nobles were provincial in every sense of the word. Service in the empire, however, could provide them with vital means to earn the money necessary to maintain status and acquire property. This went on being a consideration into the twentieth century.

Those nobles who enjoyed power and wealth tended to be nobles not only by birth, but also by inherited family position. Government sought the consent of the powerful nobles, not so much through constitutional necessity but because of its reliance on nobles as the effective administration in the community (alongside, for different purposes, the Church), and also because cooperation was seen as desirable as well as essential, a source of legitimacy as much as of implementation. Successful government initiatives were generally those that the nobility were willing to support, acquiesce in or, at least, not actively seek to thwart. The co-option of members of old noble houses, the ennoblement of non-noble officials, and the promotion in the aristocracy of low-ranking members who held important offices, helped to sustain the noble dominance of central government. The council system of government caused delay, but also permitted aristocratic representation, which in practice included non-violent opposition to policy by nobles. At the same time, John V (r. 1706–50) demonstrated his control over his nobles.

The nobles' dominance of local government was both a practical response by the Crown to the real power of the nobility in the localities, and in accordance with cultural values and ideological norms. Noble dominance of local government was important, both governmentally and politically, and took two forms: control over the relevant posts, and the allocation to the nobles of many responsibilities that might otherwise have fallen into the public sphere.

The response of the nobility to the Crown, as a whole, of particular noble families and of individual nobles was influenced by a mixture of precedent (a key element), privilege, self-interest, the interplay of traditional and novel views, and the political context. Distinctive noble status and assumptions were defined by the past: the individual past of noble birth and family status, and the collective past of grants of privileges in return for services. The aristocratic coats of arms found in many historic houses and churches exemplified the significance of status, and the extent to which it had to be displayed.

The nobility was articulated by patronage relationships and kinship, each of which were sustained by marital choice. These relationships linked the court nobility, with its social eminence and favoured access to the monarchy, to the poor provincial nobility. There was also competition for patronage, and this competition could lead to serious feuds. This struggle encompassed rivalry at court and tension in the localities.

The nobility pressed hard on the peasantry who suffered many burdens in the world of work and from feudal dues. Moreover, Portuguese agriculture was very backward, the aristocracy preferring to seek wealth through colonial and court appointments. There was no equivalent to the landlord-led 'agricultural revolution' of new techniques, notably the use in rotation of nitrogenous crops, seen in England from the sixteenth century. The lack of significant agricultural growth was more serious because, in common with the rest of Europe, there was major population growth: from 1.1 million in 1636, to 2.14 million in 1736, and 3.35 million in 1776. This put heavy pressure on living standards, and notably so in years with poor harvests. In these, Portugal had to compete with Spain for grain imports from northern Europe.

At the same time, there were also what could be termed the middling orders, middle class or bourgeoisie. In rural society, the middling order was composed of the agents of landlords and, where they existed, tenant farmers. There was a widespread aspiration among them to rise in landed society.

Towns

The middling order, those who lacked *nobreza* but were not *mecânicos*, was a key element in the urban population, but suffered from a widespread social disdain for trade. By the early eighteenth century, trade and industry was largely dominated by foreigners, although there were some local industries, such as linen at Amarante. Shipbuilding, once flourishing, was in a bad state and was dependent on foreign shipwrights. Textile production, other than in household contexts for local use, was hit hard by British imports. The vast majority of towns did not enjoy any marked growth. Many were economically and demographically dormant market centres.

Towns certainly helped to form the commercial and fiscal infrastructure that sustained more dramatic and substantial cases of growth. Yet, towns also competed, which reduced their collective political strength. Rivals for economic and other benefits, towns sought a cooperative partnership with government. Locations of administration, both state and religious, towns were centres of production, trade and consumption. Towns were in a symbiotic, but also difficult, relationship with their rural hinterlands. They were markets for their products, but also often harsh would-be controllers of the relationship, not least in the provision of loans. There were also disputes over the allocation of tax obligations.

Yet, it would be a mistake to present town and countryside simply as rivals. The clashes between them were not always as clear as they might seem, or to be regarded as town–country antagonisms. Instead, on a longstanding pattern, there were important links. Peasants flocked to towns, not only to market, a regular process, but also to attend fairs or religious ceremonies.

Towns shared in the inegalitarian and hierarchical nature of Portuguese society. The smallest group of townspeople were the wealthy and prominent, their power expressed in, and deriving from, their ability to organise others, generally economically and often politically. Their strength extended into the rural hinterland, where they would enjoy influence as a result of their power as a source of credit, tend to own estates and, if merchants, control rural industry. Within the towns, this group might be employers or landowners but, more commonly, would enjoy political power as a result of social status and its control over the institutions of urban government. Some members of the group would possess noble rank, though the importance of that varied greatly. Most derived their income from trade, official, and particularly judicial, positions, and the profits from wealth invested in land or in interest-paying loans.

As in the countryside, the largest urban group by far was the poor, the group that has left fewest signs. They lacked political weight and often were not citizens of the town in any legal sense. Their poverty stemmed from the precarious nature of much employment in even the most prosperous of towns and the absence of any effective system of social welfare. Most lacked the skills that commanded a decent wage and many had only seasonal or episodic employment. A large number were immigrants from the countryside. As a result of their poverty, the poor were very vulnerable to changes in the availability and price of food and generally lived in inadequate housing. The fit poor tended to be treated harshly, because it was assumed that they should be able to work.

In between these two groups, although not separated rigidly from them in economic terms, was a third one enjoying a more settled income than the poor. Many in this group were artisans, their economic interests and social cohesion often expressed through guilds or other fraternities of workmen. The consistent pattern of tight intermarriage within socio-economic groups (endogamy) made entry into the élite of merchants and magistracy very difficult. Artisans were generally far more socially integrated than day-labourers, servants and paupers, not least due to membership of guilds and fraternities. Municipal government and military orders excluded artisans, as did some lay confraternities. As citizenship was generally rightful membership of an urban community, such exclusions were highly significant.

Religion

This was a fearful society in which ideas of racial purity and religious conformity were enforced, not least with strict codes based on 'purity of blood'. In part, this was due to anxiety about social mobility, notably that low-borns could challenge those above. This anxiety focused on converted Jews and Muslims and on the fear that they could impersonate and pass for 'pure' Christians. Alleged crypto-Judaism was the principal target of the Inquisition, although Protestants and crypto-Muslims were also in the frame. The Jews having been expelled, the Church doubted the integrity of those who had become converts, the so-called 'New Christians'. Such ethnic and religious tensions drew on long-held anxieties and animosities. It is terribly easy to treat those killed just as numbers. The Inquisition records, however, permit the understanding of individual stories, although the records provide accounts that are refracted and distorted by the Inquisition's concerns and views. Thus, Isaac de Castro Tartas, a son of Portuguese *conversos* who in fact were crypto-Jews, settled in south-west France, was burned at the stake in Lisbon in 1647 at the age of twenty-one. Very bright, he was transcultural, being educated at the Jesuit College in Bordeaux before receiving rabbinic instruction in Amsterdam. Having travelled to Dutch Brazil, he was arrested in Portuguese Brazil to which he had travelled for unclear reasons. Deemed an apostate, he was taken to Lisbon for trial. His interrogation can be followed in the Inquisition records.

Between 1682 and 1691, 1329 'New Christians' were examined, the majority from the upper middle class. On arrest, all possessions were confiscated and the family lost its house. There could be no complaints about the Inquisition as that itself was an excommunicable crime. Questioning and torture went on for years.

Trade was hit hard by the attack on the 'New Christians'. This attack also discouraged them from keeping their capital in Portugal, and thus accentuated the movement of funds to England and the Dutch Republic. Thomas Burnet, the British Consul in Lisbon, observed in 1720: 'here are too many companys of friars and nuns to admit of other trading companies. And believe me credit and the Inquisition never lived in the same country.' British commentators were generally critical, the *Weekly Register* claiming of Portugal on 19 October 1734: 'ecclesiastical tyranny is the worst tyranny, and Hell itself not half so terrible as the Inquisition'.

There were periodical increases in the pace of persecution, as in 1671 as a result of a sacrilege in a church at Odivelas. However, inquisitorial activity diminished with time: fifty-one people were executed as a result in 1734–43 compared to eighteen in 1750–9. The Marquis of Pombal's administration was a crucial period: 1761 witnessed the last case of capital punishment, and in 1768 the distinction between 'Old' and 'New Christians' was abolished. This, however, was a legal step. The complex granulation of society saw the distinction continue to play a role.

Religion was important to the public image of the monarchy. A strong Catholic devotion was displayed, with participation in religious education, ritual and patronage all key aspects of royalty's role. At the same time, there could be discrepancies. John V had a large number of affairs and several illegitimate children, including affairs with at least three nuns. Indeed, the convent at Odivelas was the source of nuns as mistresses for many members of the élite as well as the kings, and had been so since the reign of his father, Peter.

John nevertheless was also ostentatiously devout, his devotion and wealth leaving dramatic form in the palace-monastery of Mafra, a vast work of 880 rooms covering 4 square kilometres, including a large barrel-vaulted library, begun in 1717. Completed in 1750, Mafra was constructed in accordance with his vow to build a monastery for the Franciscans if his wife became pregnant, as she did. John also paid for the Chapel of St John the Baptist that was built in Rome and reconstructed in the Church of St Roque in Lisbon, and for the large cloister of the Santa Clara convent in Coimbra. In 1716, John sent warships to help Austria and Venice against the Turks, a measure intended to influence papal opinion.

John, indeed, fulfilled a major goal in winning the rank of patriarch for the Archbishop of Lisbon in 1717, although there was some serious bullying to achieve that end. The rank of patriarch, and thus, in effect, the second cleric in Catholic Christendom after the Pope, also affected the position of the Archbishop of Braga and thereby further concentrated power and authority in Lisbon. John also won the title Most Faithful. John himself was a friend of Nuno da Cunha, the Inquisitor General from 1707 to 1750.

At the same time, there was more to John. He was interested in developments elsewhere, including in the sciences and arts, and was willing to turn to foreign experts and Portuguese who had lived abroad.

Baroque and Rococo

The key architectural style was the Baroque. A European-wide style, this, in Portugal, was the product of independence and Brazilian gold, and it thrived particularly in the eighteenth century rather than, as in Italy, in the seventeenth. Key works were ecclesiastical, such as Mafra, the Church of St Roque, the monumental staircase at *Bom Jesus do Monte*, the chancel of Évora cathedral, and the Church of Our Lady of the Rosary in Olhão, which was funded by donations from fishermen. There were also secular works, notably the stately home at Mateus, which was built in the early eighteenth century. An aspect of the culture of the period was the large collection of the relics of saints (still on display) and the substantial chapel.

Thanks to the focus on the Baroque, the Rococo (*Rocócó*) only had a limited impact. It can be seen in particular in the Palace of Queluz near Lisbon, which was built from 1747, and in the palace and gardens at Estoi in the Algarve. Queluz is a charming site, both the beautifully decorated palace itself and the gardens, which include an ornamental canal. Built for Peter, later husband of Maria I, Queluz became the residence of her son John.

Josefa de Óbidos

The Baroque is not noted for women painters, but Josefa (c. 1630–84) was prolific. Her father, a Portuguese painter from Óbidos, had trained in Seville. Josefa produced religious works, notably for churches and convents, including for the Saint Catherine altarpiece for the Church of Santa Maria in Óbidos (1661), as well as portraits and still-lifes. The latter can be found in the *Museu Nacional de Arte Antiga* in Lisbon as well as in the Municipal Library in Santarém.

War and International Relations, 1703–62

Portuguese intervention in the War of the Spanish Succession led to a renewal of Portugal's conflict with Spain. Portuguese forces were a major part of the Allied armies in Iberia. An Anglo-Portuguese force successfully besieged Franco-Spanish counterparts in Alcântara in 1706, and Madrid was occupied briefly in 1706 and 1710. However, Castilian loyalty to Philip V, and Louis XIV's support for his neighbouring grandson, proved too strong. Philip's cause became identified with national independence, despite his heavy reliance on French troops who seriously defeated the Allies at Almanza in 1707. The Portuguese cavalry and infantry fought poorly there and were driven from the field, leaving the British and Dutch infantry to be beaten by Marshal Berwick's far more numerous Franco-Spanish forces. The British frequently complained about the Portuguese as allies, prefiguring later tensions. British concerns included a fear that Portugal would not play an adequate role in campaigning in Spain, and thus that British units sent there would simply serve to protect Portugal from attack.

However, the Portuguese were willing to fight hard. Berwick, who led a Franco-Spanish force into Portugal in 1704, was surprised by the weakness of organised resistance, but equally amazed by the vigour of the peasants in attacks on his communications and in fighting back in the villages. He made minor gains on the frontier that year, but was unable to persist, in part due to pressure on Philip V's cause from the Allies in Catalonia and in southern Spain, where the British seized Gibraltar. There was another brief Spanish invasion in 1707.

The war brought dynastic recognition to the monarchy. In 1708, John V (r. 1706–50) married his cousin Maria Ana, the daughter of the Emperor Leopold I, and thus the sister of Leopold's heir, Joseph I (r. 1705–11), and of the Habsburg candidate for the throne of Spain, 'Charles III'. She was a cousin of John as Leopold's wife was Peter II's sister. Maria Ana was escorted to Portugal by British warships.

The war saw Portugal very much move to the British camp, with important economic links developing. The Methuen Treaty of 1703 opened the country for British cloth and gave Portuguese wines a considerable advantage in the British market. The French foreign minister was not wrong to argue in 1750 that the alliance between Britain and Portugal essentially stemmed from the accession of a French prince to the Spanish throne in 1700. British commercial advantages ensured that this political alignment brought important economic benefits, but the key steps in sustaining it were political. In 1761, at a time of international tension, John, 3rd Earl of Bute, George III's leading adviser, was to remark 'the safety of Portugal is most essential to the interest of this country'.

Imports of port from Portugal replaced those of claret from France. Britain's central role in Portuguese trade was widely understood by contemporaries. In 1716, a French report from Oporto claimed that three-quarters of the goods on the Portuguese ships bound for Brazil were British and that the British obtained the gold brought back from Brazil. British press reports to the same effect harmed relations with Portugal whose government was sensitive to the issue.

The *Flying-Post*, a London paper, in its issue of 25 January 1718 noted that, from the previous January to November, 180 British ships had arrived in the Douro, compared to 12 French, 9 Dutch and 20 Portuguese. The *Post Boy* of 21 February 1723 reported that the Brazil fleet was to sail from Lisbon 'having on board large quantities of woollen goods, mostly manufactured in England'. There was a sense of Portugal as an informal member of the British commercial empire, a member that was both important and vulnerable. As the *St James's Journal* of 23 February 1723 pointed out, 'whatever their laws may be against our carrying away their gold from Portugal, our merchants have always understood the Portuguese to be only their factors for bringing it to them from the Indies'. Portuguese gold coins circulated in England.

However, British diplomats did not necessarily appreciate Portugal. Brigadier James Dormer, who had served in Iberia in the War of the Spanish Succession, liked the Lisbon climate but found the entertainment dull. Sent out in 1725, he was recalled in 1727 after instigating an attack on the British consul, Thomas Burnet. Another veteran of the Iberian campaigns in the War of the Spanish Succession, James, 2nd Lord Tyrawly, ambassador from 1727 to 1741, frequently sought a move, William, 2nd Earl of Albemarle observing in 1732 that Tyrawly was tired of his post, 'and indeed I do not wonder at it for in this world there never was so detestable a place [Lisbon], no company, no diversions, a little stinking town filled with bugs and vermin'. Glad to leave, Albemarle found Seville much nicer. Tyrawly compensated for his boredom with an active sex life. The anonymous *Present State of Germany* claimed in 1738: 'the capital of Portugal is such a cut-throat place, that few strangers, except such as are in the retinue of public ministers, dare trust themselves on land, but retire to the vessels on the river at night'.

Alongside close economic links, Britain in 1735 sent a large fleet to the Tagus to protect Portugal from threatened Spanish attack, a fleet that stayed there until 1737. However, there were tensions. In 1723, the Portuguese destroyed the British Royal African Company's base in Cabinda, and clashes over the region continued late into the century. In 1729, Tyrawly pressed for a firm response to Portugal in a commercial dispute, arguing that it was impracticable for Portugal 'to do anything that can prevent a squadron of the King's [George II's] ships from coming to an anchor at the King's [John V's] palace, whenever His Majesty [George II] pleases'. Indeed, Tyrawly wanted every squadron sent to the Mediterranean to visit Lisbon 'for these people are not to be trusted longer than the rod is held over them'.

In contrast, the British response was usually cautious. In 1726, when Infante Francisco, the Duke of Beja, a son of Peter II, approached Dormer, he told him that his brother, John V, was pro-Spanish and suggested that Britain, then in dispute with Spain, intimidate Portugal with a powerful fleet, the British did not respond. Indeed, Francisco was interested in replacing his brother. In 1729, in response to Tyrawly, Thomas, Duke of Newcastle, the Secretary of State for the Southern Department, urged compromise, arguing that the importance of the Portuguese trade to Britain was accentuated by Anglo-Spanish differences. Moreover, that was the year of a double marriage between two of John's children, including his heir, and two of Philip V of Spain, including his heir.

Portugal certainly let Britain down. Portugal did not join Britain in its next war with Spain, the War of Jenkins' Ear (1739–48). So also with the Seven Years War, in which Britain went to war with France in 1756. At the same time, Portuguese vulnerability was a key issue. John V pointed out to Tyrawly in 1735 that the British fleet could not protect Portugal from land attack. Meanwhile, there was a degree of administrative change. A separate office for foreign affairs was created in 1736, although it had been considered desirable earlier.

There was no vogue for British constitutionalism, literature, science, attitudes or fashion in Portugal, as there was across much of Europe. This was not simply due to religious differences, for in Catholic France there was much interest in such spheres of British life. Instead, the difference reflected the greater strength of Counter-Reformation ideology and Baroque preferences in Portugal.

At the same time, Portugal had no serious territorial claims on any other European power. Her dynastic diplomacy was not intended as a means to gain German or Italian territories. Boxed in by Spain, the Braganzas had no tradition of international aggrandisement through such diplomacy, nor of ruling non-contiguous European territories. This was no equivalent to the house of Hanover ruling Britain. In addition, the wars of the first two decades of the century had not left Portugal with the impetus for revanchist policies, as they had left Spain and Sweden.

The Portuguese shared this limited interest in European (as opposed to colonial) territorial aggrandisement with the British. In that, both powers compared with the United Provinces (Dutch Republic) and contrasted markedly with most other European states. As a result, Portuguese aims posed less of a problem for British alliance diplomacy than those of other powers. These limited aims helped to ensure relatively good peacetime political relations. However, precisely because of them Portugal was disinclined to follow Britain's lead when it came to war, and would not back the British practice of intervening in European diplomacy. This contrast continued into the twentieth century.

The Empire

The Portuguese were very much passed and left further behind by as an imperial power in this period by England, the Dutch, France and Spain, with their territorial expansion essentially restricted to the interior of Brazil. Portugal's empire was dynamic neither in Asia nor in Africa during the eighteenth century, but the situation was very different in South America.

Tomatoes from Portugal

Lord Tyrawly wrote from Lisbon in 1733:

> I don't know that I have any other vegetable worth send-ing you, except tomatoes, which is a large round fruit, as big as a small orange (of which I believe you have none in England). It is not to be eaten, by itself, yet comes within your rule of having nothing but belly timber, for if your cook scalds them first in hot water, four or five of them, or more, or less according as you like the last, or without scalding, put them whole into your soup, provided that it stands afterwards, time enough to mitonner, it will as we think here, much mend your soup, by giving it a far more agreeable tartness, than sorrel, or any other herb. It grows up a tall shrub, with many leaves, the fruit, being when ripe, as red as a cherry.

Native to western South America, tomatoes had been grown in England from the 1590s, but were believed poisonous or at least unfit for eating, and it was not until the mid-eigh-teenth century that they became widely eaten there.

In Africa, having lost Mombasa to the Omanis in 1698 after a long siege, the Portuguese regained it in 1728, but lost it anew in 1729 as a result of low morale and problems with food supplies, and another attempt to regain the city failed in 1769. However, Delagoa Bay, lost to the Dutch in 1720, was regained in 1730. The Portuguese lost Mazagão to Morocco in 1765. In Central Africa, Portuguese policy had shifted away in the 1680s from large-scale wars aimed at conquest, a reflection of the serious difficulties experienced in Angola and the Zambezi Valley.

In India, the Portuguese were hard pressed in 1737–40 when they were involved in a disastrous war with the Marathas, who benefited from the support of disaffected peasantry. They provided an infantry to complement the Maratha cavalry, and this infantry was crucial to successful sieges: Salsette fell in 1737, Bassein in 1739 and Chaul in 1740, although Goa, the key position, held out when attacked in 1739. Portugal was fortunate that, thanks to their alliance in Europe, Goa was not the target for British attacks, unlike the French bases in India.

Whereas, in the late sixteenth century, the Portuguese had perhaps been the first of the Europeans to explore Australia, their position was taken over by the Dutch in the seventeenth and by the British in the eighteenth. The Portuguese role in the Newfoundland fisheries declined.

Brazil

In Brazil, major discoveries of gold in Minas Gerais in 1693–5 encouraged further expansion into the interior. The flow of gold to Portugal expanded rapidly. Indeed, a British diplomat recorded in 1723 that the fleet from Rio de Janeiro arrived in Lisbon with a 'considerable quantity of unregistered gold'. The shape of Portuguese Brazil changed greatly. Captaincies (provinces) were founded for São Paulo (1709), Minas Gerais (1720), Goiás (1744) and Mato Grosso (1748), while Brazil became a viceroyalty in 1760. Gold provided a major new stimulus for the slave trade, increasing both demand for slaves and a source of payment for them. Slaves worked in the mines and in tasks such as washing diamond-bearing rocks: diamonds were discovered in the Serro do Frio area in the 1720s. Aside from in Minas Gerais, where the towns of Minas Novas and Diamantina were founded in 1727 and 1730 respectively, there was also gold deposits in Cuiabá (1719), Goiás and Mato Grosso.

The sugar plantations of north-east Brazil declined in importance from the 1710s, as competing sugar production from the

West Indies became more important. Cacao production from the late 1670s did not compensate. However, from the late eighteenth century, sugar and coffee plantations near Rio de Janeiro became prominent, and the city replaced Bahia as capital of Brazil in 1763. Cotton (from the 1760s) and tobacco were also significant exports from Brazil, and there were over one million slaves there by 1800. The Portuguese slave-owners in Brazil preferred to import adult male slaves rather than to encourage slave families, and, combined with the physical strain of the work and a high mortality rate, this practice ensured a continual need for more slaves, as well as a slave population that remained close to its African roots. Angola supplied about two million slaves during the century, mostly to Brazil, and the Portuguese also had slave bases further north, especially in Portuguese Guinea. Food and clothing for the slaves on the plantations was inadequate, and the work was remorseless, hard and long. The conditions of work for pregnant women led to many stillbirths, while, through poor diet, mothers lacked sufficient milk.

Control over the slaves did not prevent opposition in many forms, although it was generally unsuccessful unless in the shape of flight. As a result of the latter, there were organised communities of fugitive slaves. Rebellion, in contrast, failed. A revolt in Salvador in 1798 called for the abolition of slavery, but was suppressed in the context of white fear. The control over Brazil ensured the flow of resources that produced the revenues for such works as Mafra.

Although most slaves came from Angola, with a fifty-day sailing from Luanda to Rio de Janeiro, slave raiding was still practised in Brazil at the expense of the native people and did much to hit their numbers. Native slaves and forced labour were important in Amazonia for the collection of cacao, sarsaparilla and other forest products, but, in 1743–9, possibly half the native population of the Amazon Valley fell victim to measles and smallpox.

Slave raiding was resisted by the *reducciones*, frontier settlements under Jesuit supervision where native people grew crops. However, in 1756, a joint Portuguese-Spanish army used firepower to smash native opposition as they advanced on these missions. As a result, the Brazilian border fixed by Portugal and Spain in the Treaty of Madrid in 1750 was enforced. This border awarded these missions to Portugal as part of a westward extension of the 1494 delimitation under the Treaty of Tordesillas.

At the same time, Portuguese firepower could only achieve so much. A convoy of gold seekers in canoes was destroyed by the Paiaguá on the River Paraguay in 1725, and another was mauled the following year. The Paiaguá fired their bows more rapidly than the Portuguese their muskets, and they also made masterly use of their canoes, not least by leaping into the water and tipping them up to protect themselves from musket fire. In 1730, the annual flotilla carrying gold was ambushed and mostly destroyed on the way back from Cuiabá. Punitive Portuguese expeditions achieved little in 1730 and 1731, but in 1734 the combination of surprise attack and firepower devastated the Paiaguá. Although the latter mounted successful attacks in 1735 and 1736, their casualties led to a slackening of activity, and they were also affected by disease and by the attacks of the Guaicurú, a rival tribe. By the 1780s, the Paiaguá had been largely wiped out, but their story shows the danger of assuming a simple model of European military superiority.

Elsewhere, the use of native allies was important. Portuguese troops were unable to defeat the Caiapó, who ambushed settlers and convoys, but the Bororo, in contrast, under the leadership of a Portuguese woodsman, António Pires de Campos, pressed the Caiapó hard in a bitter war between 1745 and 1751. The Portuguese ability to win and exploit local allies reflected the lack of native unity. This, disease and the consequences of enslavement all helped the Portuguese far more than any success in contact warfare.

In Amazonia, the Portuguese advance up the River Tapajós was resisted by the Mawé, while, in the 1760s and 1770s, the Portuguese were unable to resist guerrilla attacks by the mobile Mura with their ambushes of Portuguese canoes and their attacks on isolated settlements. The Mura were highly effective with their bows and arrows, and the peace they agreed in 1784 was an accommodation, not a capitulation.

Meanwhile, Portuguese migration to Brazil totalled perhaps close to one million in the century as a whole. This was a lower figure than that from the enforced migration of slaves, but it was one that was to be highly important politically. As with the cases of British North America in the 1770s and Spanish America in the 1810s, this growth of a settler population was to be the basis for political assertiveness in the 1820s.

Gold, Portugal and Britain

Control over Brazil was the basis for the vast wealth being brought into Portugal, and helped account for the country's international importance. It also left Portugal vulnerable to a breakdown in the imperial relationship with Brazil. This was more so than Britain with what became the United States, as the British also had a strong position in India; one, indeed, that from the late seventeenth century and, even more, early eighteenth was stronger than that of Portugal there.

Britain was dependent on the gold that flowed in from the credit balance in Anglo-Portuguese trade. In what was essentially a metallic trading system, Britain was short of specie and greatly in need of Brazilian gold. This was true not only for British trade with areas such as the Baltic and the Orient, which were characterised, in general, by a negative trade balance, but also for British foreign policy which depended, especially in wartime, on providing subsidies to continental allies. Thus, in 1742, as Britain prepared for entry into the War of the Austrian Succession, a leading London banker and merchant, Thomas Gore, informed Spencer, Earl of Wilmington, the First Lord of the Treasury, that the best way to move funds to pay the subsidy promised to Austria was by moving gold from Lisbon to Trieste or Genoa. Gore added, 'I can supply funds and credits at Lisbon sufficient to answer this service.'

The Cape Verde Islands

Portuguese from the fifteenth century, the Cape Verde Islands were a waystation on maritime routes to Africa, the Indian Ocean and South America. Visiting in 1702, Francis Rogers commented on Praia: 'a fine, fruitful, plentiful island, but hot, most of whose inhabitants are a sort of banditti (or banished, transported for crimes) or thieves, as an abundance of our countrymen can witness when they touched there for water or fresh provisions'. In 1669, Captain John Narbrough noted 'very good fresh water', but people 'much given to thievery'. Maize and bananas were grown. Now, very differently, tourism began in the 1970s on the island of Sal, and rose to over 716,000 tourists in 2017; 23 per cent were from Britain and 11.2 per cent from Germany. The Portuguese mainland was the third largest source of tourists that year. Benefiting from a lack of rainfall, the tourists' focus is on the sandy beaches of the islands of Sal, Boa Vista and Maio.

8. Earthquakes: Physical and Political, 1750–1807

Divine judgement, that was the general view on the Lisbon earthquake of 1755, which was a truly European catastrophe. A sweeping tsunami that followed a shattering offshore earthquake of about 9 on the Richter scale, first appeared to empty the Tagus and, then, produced a flood that overcame much of the city on 1 November, All Saints' Day. Uncontrollable fires, many owing to candles lit in the churches for the services of that day, contributed to the chaos. In Lisbon, many people were killed. Moreover, thanks to the three shocks from the earthquake, the fires and the flood, about 85 per cent of the buildings were destroyed, including the royal palace and its library, paintings and archives, as well as the Royal Hospital of All Saints, the Patriarchate, the Jesuit College and the Inquisition.

In about 1740, Matthäus Seutter, a major German mapmaker, produced an engraved map of Lisbon. He described it as magnificent and as a flourishing emporium, and his map depicted not only monasteries, churches and palaces, but also a river with many ships. Much of what he showed, however, was devastated in 1755.

That was not the sole damage. In the Algarve, close to the epicentre, there was also terrible devastation from the earthquake and the tsunami, for example in Faro, as also in the Azores. The impact was felt much more extensively, but it was most apparent to the world at Lisbon. The British rushed to provide charitable support.

The devastation proved a spiritual challenge, a challenge that had political consequences. In 1761, Gabriel Malagrida, an Italian

Jesuit preacher who had been regarded as a prophet and a saint in Portugal, and who had attributed the earthquake to divine anger with the Portuguese government, was publicly garrotted and burnt. This dramatic act expressed the power of the government, but also its anxieties.

The Secretary of State of Foreign Affairs and War, Sebastião José de Carvalho e Melo (1699–1782), from 1770 the Marquis of Pombal, responded promptly and ably to the crisis caused by the earthquake, for example by hanging looters, winning the favour of Joseph I (1750–77) and becoming secretary of state of internal affairs (in effect the prime minister) on 6 May 1756. Born in 1699, the son of a country squire, he had worked his way up by his talent and energy. In 1749, John V's wife, Maria Ana, had him recalled from his embassy in Vienna to become Secretary of State for Foreign Affairs. Pombal's position, energy and ambitions were a threat to the prominent aristocrats. This encouraged Pombal's rivals among the aristocracy to drastic means.

The attempted assassination of the King on 3 September 1758, on his way back from visiting his favourite mistress, Teresa, wife of Luis Bernardo, heir of the Távora family, created a crisis that ended on 13 January 1759 with the public execution of many of the prestigious Távora family and its relatives, sixteen in all. They were accused of high treason and attempted regicide, including of plotting to put the Duke of Aveiro on the throne. He was among those executed. Leonor, Marchioness of Távora, who was also among those executed, was a devout Catholic. Malagrida, her confessor, was among those arrested. The mistress was her daughter-in-law. Although the Távoras and Joseph indeed had poor relations, the crime and its aftermath were convenient for Pombal and there is considerable doubt about what actually happened and why. Joseph, who had been wounded in the shooting, was present to watch the executions, and he, rather than Pombal, may have been responsible for the severity of the punishments.

Pombal followed up by expelling the Jesuits in September 1759. Pro-government writings denounced Jesuitical subversion. In France, the Jesuits had been blamed, without cause, for the attempted assassination of Louis XV in 1757. Suspicious of Jesuit intentions in their South American missions, the *reducciones*, and concerned about their power in Portugal, Pombal had become convinced that the Jesuits had to be destroyed. Diplomatic relations with the papacy were severed in 1760–9 when there was dissatisfaction with papal support for the Jesuits. The government took over control of censorship in 1768, but this did not necessarily entail a weakening of the Catholic position within Portugal. Clerics continued to play a role and non-Catholic doctrines were still censored.

Meanwhile, Joseph continued his hobby of hunting, notably at the extended palace at Salvaterra, a major hunting lodge. An opera house was installed so that he could indulge his other hobby. Allegedly the Queen, Mariana Victoria of Spain, had ugly ladies in waiting in order to restrain another of the King's interests. Joseph had views, and Pombal had to heed them, but Joseph was not really interested in being an active monarch. In essentials, the two men agreed, notably in wishing to restrains the independence of the greater nobles and the Church. The Grand Inquisitor, Joseph's half-brother, and another of the half-brothers were exiled from court from 1760 to 1777 because they clashed with Pombal.

War, 1762

Another crisis followed swiftly. In 1762, when the Seven Years War (1756–63) broadened out to include Spain on France's side against Britain, Spain attacked Portugal in order to put pressure on Britain to compensate for losses elsewhere. Indeed, the British conquered Manila and Havana from Spain that year.

Reasons for British Intervention in Portugal

On 30 January 1762, the British *Monitor* reported: 'If Holland and Portugal should fall to the arms of the Bourbon family, their connections in the East Indies will follow, and enable the French . . . to destroy our interest and property in those countries. The addition of the gold and diamonds from Brazil and Congo will supply the wants of every force they shall keep on foot.'

Portugal had hitherto been neutral and, in 1759, had bitterly complained when British warships entered Portuguese waters at Lagos in order to finish off a French fleet en route to take part in an invasion attempt, in what was the largest naval battle to occur off mainland Portugal. In May 1762, the invading Spanish forces had some success, overrunning weak and poorly defended fortresses such as Bragança, Chaves and Miranda. The explosion of the powder magazine in the castle of besieged Miranda did much damage and killed about 400 people. Almeida was to share this fate when besieged by the French in 1810.

This crisis led to urgent requests for British troops, requests that won support from the British government and much public backing, although there were British diplomats who thought Portugal defenceless and this view was also expressed in the press. After being delayed by contrary winds in the Channel in late June, a British expeditionary force, 7104 strong, helped to stiffen the Portuguese defence. In the face of effective guerrilla opposition, the Spanish failure to exploit their early successes by a march on Oporto was crucial and led to anger in Spain, where the general, Nicolás, Marquis of Sarriá, was replaced.

In July, a second invasion, by French and Spanish forces, was mounted, leading to the fall of Almeida. However, deployed east of Abrantes, British and Portuguese troops helped block the invasion. Guerrilla attacks on Spanish supply lines and a scorched earth policy also hit the invaders. On 27 August, the British and Portuguese struck back, capturing the Spanish supply base at Valencia de Alcántara, with John Burgoyne playing a key role. That August, the Duc de Choiseul, the French foreign minister, decided that the moment had been lost for the conquest of Portugal. Despite the problems they faced, the British forces operated effectively and, on 5 October, stormed the entrenched Spanish camp of Vila Velha, inflicting heavy casualties. Facing the onset of the winter rains, the imminence of peace and the strength of the British presence, the Franco-Spanish troops retreated. In November, the Spaniards advanced again, only to be repelled from the fortified positions at Marvão and Ouguela on 9–10 November.

On 15 November, the Spaniards retreated and a week later they asked for a truce. Peace was negotiated in 1763 without Portugal or Spain gaining any territory from each other on their frontier. In modern south-western Uruguay, Spain returned *Colonia del Sacramento*, a Portuguese position established in 1680 over which the two powers had long struggled, with Spanish attacks successful in 1680, 1705 and 1762.

Portugal in 1762

The correspondence of the British commanders throws light on the country in this period. In July, Brigadier Frederick provided a depressing account of the logistical problems he faced on the march to Santarém, which in part arose from the poverty of the region. He found no beef or bread prepared for his troops, and it proved impossible to obtain adequate supplies:

> all the bread that the magistrate said he could possibly get before they marched was two hundred small loaves

which was so small a quantity, it was impossible to divide amongst the men. I ordered the regiment to march the next morning at half an hour past three, but the carriages for the baggage not coming at the proper time it was past six before they began their march. It was late in the day before they got to Santarem when Colonel Biddulph reported to me that by the excessive heat and sandy roads that above half the regiment had dropped behind and was afraid many of the men would die, on which surgeons were sent to their assistance . . . at Santarem . . . the men were lying in the streets, the inhabitants had shut up their houses, and the magistrates had provided no quarters for them, neither was there beef or bread for the men . . . they were fainting with the heat and want of food . . . nine men of the Buffs died on the march yesterday.

Lord Tyrawly, formerly the British ambassador in Lisbon and now returned as both ambassador and general, complained that the troops had neither straw nor beds, and that the shelter and bread supplied were inadequate. There were also serious problems with communications. Captain Fraser Folliott found a supposed ford over the Tagus was five feet deep in water and the current very rapid, while the roads nearby were impassable for wheeled vehicles.

Pombal and Reform

For Pombal, change was essential. He wished not to destroy the old nobility, but to revive it by an infusion of new blood and thus create a governing group open to new ideas and aware of the value of trade. As a former Portuguese envoy to Britain and then Austria, he was aware of other ways of doing things. In London, to which he was appointed in 1738, he had been elected a Fellow of the Royal Society and had taken an interest in British economic developments.

During Pombal's period in office (1750–77), the Enlightenment coincided in Portugal with the struggle of an old power to be great again, by adopting and adapting self-consciously the techniques its government believed its competitors had used to surpass Portugal. Far more successfully than John V, who had tried to encourage industry, for example by establishing a paper manufacturing industry at Lousã, Pombal sought to pursue an economic nationalism that would bring freedom from foreign influence. Thus, he supported large merchants in their disputes with their smaller competitors, because he saw the latter as commission agents for the foreign merchant he hoped to displace with the assistance of the former. So also with his foundation of chartered trading companies to profit from the Brazilian economy and limit the role of British merchants. In 1756, in addition, Pombal created the General Company of Agriculture and Alto Douro Vines in order to regulate the production and marketing of Douro wines. This was on the model of the Hungarian measures to ensure the quality of Tokaj wine. The headquarters, built in Régua, are the basis of the impressive Douro museum established in 1997.

Due to Pombal's economic nationalism, Anglo-Portuguese relations deteriorated, but the growth in the Portuguese economy was apparent. In 1767, the British envoy in Paris reported that the French were hopeful of gaining some of the Anglo-Portuguese trade. The *Present State of Europe*, in its issue of January 1730, noted that 301 of the 534 merchant ships that came into Lisbon in 1729 were British (71 were Portuguese and 54 French). In contrast, the list of arrivals in 1787 published in the *Morning Herald* of 28 January 1788 showed that 332 of the 1045 were British, but 300 were Portuguese.

Lisbon was successfully rebuilt and in accordance with Pombal's plan for a grid of parallel streets in the Baixa (lower town) between the waterfront and the square of Rossio. The streets were matched by uniform buildings, while, in the *Praça do Comércio*, the centrepiece of the plan at the Tagus end, a still-impressive major equestrian statue of Joseph I by Machado de Castro was erected in 1775. Joseph himself had expressed his gratitude to Pombal by building in 1760 the *Igreja da Mémoria* in Belém, a Neoclassical church that contains Pombal's tomb.

The reform of the educational system was part of Pombal's policy of modernisation. In 1772, he added mathematics and natural sciences to the syllabus at Coimbra, which led to the creation there of Portugal's largest botanical gardens, 50 acres of calm pleasure and the opportunity today to see many plants from the lands of the former empire. Many of Pombal's ideas were very different to past practice. Slavery was abolished as were *autos-da-fé* and the idea of purity of blood that had served as the basis for prejudice against former Jews. In 1761, Asian and East African Christian subjects of the Portuguese Crown were given the same legal and social status as Portuguese whites on the grounds that subjects should not be distinguished by colour. It was made a criminal offence for whites to insult coloured subjects. Repeated in 1763, these regulations were given teeth when new officials were sent to Goa in 1774 with instructions to favour Indian clerics. Pombal explicitly cited the classical Roman model for colonisation: citizenship was to bring equality. If, however, there was no question of giving other religious and ethnic groups equal status, there was little different from the position in Europe where the rights of heterodox Christians or of Jews were generally limited.

Pombal was in a far stronger position in Portugal after 1759 than comparable French reforming ministers, such as René Augustin de Maupeou, the first minister from 1770 to 1774, and his policies could be radical, as with the secularisation of the Inquisition and his commercial strategies. Nevertheless, many policies had to be modified to suit local circumstances. Moreover, although when Pombal was able to give problems his complete attention, the government performed with efficiency and achieved results, such oversight was not always possible.

Furthermore, dependent on royal support, Pombal confronted the central problem that faced *ancien régime* reformers, that of perpetuating the reforms he had initiated. When Joseph I died in 1777, Pombal's position became untenable due to the hostility of Maria I. Similarly, Maupeou fell soon after the death of Louis XV.

All comparisons face problems, both conceptual and practical, not least those across time. However, there were points of comparison between Pombal and the twentieth-century Prime Minister António de Oliveira Salazar. Each was authoritarian and ready to use force against opponents. Indeed, each ultimately rested on the power of what was a police state by the standards of the age. Each gained power as a result of anger with a preceding system that appeared not fit for purpose. To avoid crisis, each wanted to avoid war abroad. Both Pombal and Salazar sought reform, and each, in a way, were political economists, but neither was able to accept alternative definitions of reform. Each pursued what were in essence corporatist solutions, and also wanted to strengthen the empire.

At the same time, there were important contrasts. By the standards of the age, Pombal was at the cutting-edge intellectually. He wanted to reduce the political power and potential of the Church, notably of the Jesuits and the Inquisition. This was not alien to the anti-clericalism of the Republicans in the 1910s. Salazar, in contrast, was very much a supporter of the clergy and, although a distinguished economist, was not otherwise at the cutting-edge intellectually. It is obviously only a thought-exercise, but it can be difficult to see Salazar moderating the race laws or moving against the Inquisition as Pombal did. As a key context for his exposition of change, Salazar was a staunch traditionalist.

However, Pombal proved a suitable point of reference. In 1934, under Salazar, the monument to Pombal in the *Praça Marquês de Pombal* or Rotunda in Lisbon was unveiled. The base of the monument referred to Pombal's reforms. Ironically, the idea for the monument had been Republican. The Republicans wanted to pay tribute to Pombal's anti-Jesuitism. However, Salazar built the statue to honour Pombal's political strength and concern to revive state and empire. Salazar depicted himself as a sort of prime minister like Pombal.

British Travellers

Tourism in Iberia long caused curiosity, as the wealthy aristocrat Charles, 2nd Duke of Richmond, discovered in 1728. His fellow aristocrat, Charles, 2nd Viscount Townshend, Secretary of State for the Northern Department, could not 'well conceive what curiosity should lead his Grace so much out of the usual road of travellers'. Tyrawly, envoy in Lisbon, wrote to Richmond: 'Point du point I think Spain and Portugal excite one's curiosity more than any other countries, as being the least known, and quite out of the Old John Trott beaten, pack horse road of all travellers, and will make you as famous to later posterity as Dampier, Sir John Mandeville, Hackluyt or Fernão Mendes Pinto,' all famed travellers.

Portugal was not regarded as the most interesting country to visit. Lisbon lacked the cosmopolitan, accessible culture of Paris, and its society was perceived as dull and reclusive. Catholicism in Portugal was more clearly anti-Protestant than in France. Language was also a barrier, with very few foreigners knowing Portuguese, although some Portuguese aristocrats spoke French. Outside Lisbon, there appeared to be little to see. There was no vogue for the beach, the mountains lacked the splendour and glamour of the Alps, the Roman antiquities were much less well known than those of Italy, and there was little interest in the Moorish remains.

Portugal was distant from Britain, although less so than Italy. The standard route was by sea. Travelling to Portugal, however, was difficult, although there was a packet boat service between Lisbon and Falmouth. Brigadier James Dormer was detained by contrary winds at Plymouth while on the way to Lisbon in 1725. On his return in December 1727, Dormer was again held by contrary winds at Lisbon for several days and the eventual voyage to Plymouth took twelve days. The following March, his replacement was delayed for fifteen days by contrary winds. The alternative, travel by land via France and Spain, was very long, involved a passage of the Pyrenees, and suffered from poor facilities for travellers, notably in Spain. Those going to the Mediterranean by sea usually called at Lisbon, John Swinton leaving a good account in his journal of his visit in 1730 – he was accosted by a pimp who offered him men or women. However, the trip across the Bay of Biscay was not always a comfortable one. Ships lacked stabilisers.

Many who went to Portugal were enthusiastic travellers, including Richmond and Henry, 3rd Earl of Radnor in 1729, and Henry, 10th Earl of Pembroke in 1786. Moreover, travel accounts were published, William Dalrymple's *Travels through Spain and Portugal in 1774* appearing in 1775. Dalrymple served in the 1762 campaign. In 1774, he was between periods of military service in North America. Other works published in London included John Colbatch's *An Account of the Court of Portugal under Pedro II* (1700), William Bromley's *Several Years Travel through Portugal, Spain, Italy, Germany, Prussia, Sweden, Denmark and the United Provinces* (1702), Joseph Baretti's *A Journey from London to Genoa, through England, Portugal, Spain and France* (1770), Richard Twiss's *Travels through Spain and Portugal in 1772 and 1773* (1775), Arthur Costigan's *Sketches of Society and Manners in Portugal* (1787), James Murphy's *Travels in Portugal in 1789 and 1790* (1795), Richard Croker's *Travels through several provinces of Spain and Portugal* (1799) and Henry Link's *Travels in Portugal* (1801). Colbatch was a doctor, Bromley a member of the landed gentry who went on to be a secretary of state. The wealthy son of an English merchant, Twiss was much travelled. Moreover, Portuguese history was staged in London in 1775 when Robert Jephson's play *Braganza: A Tragedy* was performed at the Theatre Royal in Drury Lane.

British travellers to Portugal went for a variety of reasons. Thomas Benson, MP for Barnstaple, fled there in 1753 after his fraud was discovered: facing a heavy bill for unpaid duties on tobacco, he arranged for his ship, the *Nightingale*, which had been heavily insured, to be scuttled in the Bristol Channel, her cargo having been previously unloaded on Lundy Island, which he had leased. Benson died in Portugal in 1772. Very differently, the young David Garrick, later a famous actor, went to Portugal to acquire commercial experience.

An increasing number travelled from Britain to Lisbon for reasons of health, the air and climate being regarded as among the best in Europe. The Reverend William Cole, a Cambridge antiquarian, went to Lisbon for his health in 1737, and visited Mafra and Sintra. Many, however, found death rather than recovery: Henry Fielding in 1754, Elizabeth, Marchioness of Tavistock in 1768, Patrick Moran on his passage from Bristol in 1769, William Montagu MP in 1774 and Lord John Pelham Clinton in 1781. The British cemetery in Lisbon contains several of the graves, including that of Fielding.

There was very little travel in Portugal outside Lisbon, except for those going to Madrid who tended to follow the main road via Badajoz, earning the description 'I never underwent more hardship in travelling' in 1729; while, in 1775, Thomas Pelham, later 2nd Earl of Chichester, observed, 'my journey from Lisbon has taught me all the *desagrements* and how many of them are only imaginary ones, for after two or three days travelling you fancy your boiled chicken or rabbit better than all the . . . ragouts from a French kitchen'.

Facilities for travellers outside Lisbon were, indeed, poorly developed. Travelling to Oporto in 1700, Richard Creed found the roads 'very rough' and complained: 'The worst dog kennel in England is a palace in comparison to the best inn I saw on this road. No bed in any inn. The inns generally have two rooms; one for the passengers and the other for the mules . . . everybody carry all their provisions with them.' In 1760, John, 7th Earl of Strathmore and his Cambridge contemporary, Thomas Pitt, 1st Lord Camelford, the nephew of William Pitt the Elder, travelled around Portugal before journeying on to Madrid. Plagued with poor health, Pitt began his foreign travels at Lisbon, an obvious point of departure for foreign travel when much of the Continent was rendered problematic by the Seven Years War. His aunt Anne was very unhappy about the idea of his travelling in Iberia:

> What disturbs me the most is the dreadful journey he is taking in the hottest part of the year, in the hottest part of the hottest country in Europe, after his experience in Lisbon where I find he was ill again of the complaint he had almost got the better of . . . it makes me sick to think of all he is exposing himself to, as I really think his journey must be a greater fatigue and a greater danger than a [military] campaign.

Eating in 1760

Honoured guests, thanks to a royal order, Strathmore and Pitt did not appreciate the lavish meal offered them at the great monastery of Alcobaça:

> We found a large table groaning under a service of monstrous dishes. The first we tasted was a soup composed of gravy, bad oil, vinegar and sugar: the other dishes were pyramids of boiled fowls smothered in rice; others with their limbs distorted, as if they had been spitted alive; and everything breathing garlic, saffron and bad oil. In our 2nd course we had pyramids of meat pies strewed with sugar, and ragouts powdered with spices . . . The dessert consisted of vast piles of oranges, sweet lemons, citrons and sweetmeats that disdained to owe their flavour to anything but the sugar cane.

More famously, William Beckford, who left Britain in 1785 as a result of a homosexual scandal with a young boy, visited Portugal in 1787 en route to his plantations in Jamaica, a journey he did not in the event pursue. The British envoy stopped Beckford from being introduced at court in Lisbon. Indeed, he had to leave Portugal due to his scandalous reputation. Returning to Portugal in 1793–7, he enthused about wild and primitive Portuguese scenery and land-scaped the gardens at Monserrate near Sintra, gardens praised in *Childe Harold's Pilgrimage* (1812) by George, Lord Byron, another visitor. During his later visit, Beckford visited Alcobaça and Batalha in 1794, and in 1835 published a witty, if not caustic, account of the luxurious living of the Portuguese monks, one characterised, in his account, by gluttony and sloth. He also noted the problems of travel. For example, of the valley of the Tagus: 'We were beginning to experience the effects of heat rather oppressively, when we entered a forest of pine, and felt much invigorated by fragrant, genial breezes.' Robert Southey also visited Portugal in the early 1790s. The French Revolution had disrupted established tourist routes.

Maria I

Joseph's successor, Maria I (r. 1777–1816), Maria 'the Pious', was declared insane in 1792 and her son, John, later her successor John VI, took over the government, although he only took the title of Prince Regent in 1799. In 1760, Maria had married her uncle Peter, the younger brother of her father. In 1777, they became nominally co-rulers, but the regal authority was vested solely in Maria as she was the lineal heir. A reactionary, she dismissed Pombal, and he was banished from Lisbon to his home estate at Pombal, dying in 1782.

Maria, however, suffered from melancholia, and her mental health deteriorated, notably in 1786 when Peter died, and, from 1788, when her eldest son, Joseph, died and, even more, in 1789 with the, to her, 'terrifying' news of the French Revolution which menaced her world. The contrast with Britain was clearly seen

with the role of parliament there in seeking to handle the constitutional issues arising from the ill-health of George III, which
became a major issue in 1788-9.

Portugal at Ease

In 1773, Thomas Walpole, the British envoy from 1771 to
1800, was able to write from Lisbon: 'we have here so little
connections with quarrelsome powers, that we are con-
tented with the events, and do no trouble ourselves much
with speculations: Jesuits and trade are the only objects of
politics in this corner.' Twenty years later, the situation was
to be much more disturbing.

Maria's tomb is in the Basilica of Estrela in Lisbon, which itself
was begun in 1779 on her orders in gratitude for the birth of
Joseph who, however, died of smallpox before its completion in
1790. The extent to which most monarchs left a building is a
striking feature of monarchical status and, thanks to its colonial
revenues, Portugal had the wealth to do so.

Royalty and wealth were also linked in other instances. The
incorrupt corpse of the nun Mafalda (c. 1195-1256), a daughter of
Sancho I, was discovered in 1616 and she was beatified in 1793.
Over the previous century, the convent of Arouca, which she had
endowed, had been richly redecorated and extended. It can be
visited today.

Crises with France and Spain

Portuguese relations with Britain deteriorated under Maria. In
1782, Portugal joined the League of the Armed Neutrality, a
Russian-led alliance (short of war) against Britain during the War

of American Independence that was designed to stop Britain controlling maritime trade. In 1783, France negotiated a trade treaty

---

Exploration in Africa

In 1798, Francisco Lacerda e Almeida, governor of Sena on the River Zambezi, who was concerned about the British conquest of Cape Colony from the Dutch in 1796, decided that the Portuguese needed to link their colonies of Mozambique and Angola. He reached Lake Mweru in central Africa, but died of disease there. This was the end of the attempt; although, in 1806–11, two Portuguese half-caste slave traders, Pedro Baptista and Antonio Nogueira da Rocha, crossed Africa from Cassange in Angola to Sena.

---

with Portugal. Seven years later, Portugal did not back Britain in the Nootka Sound Crisis, when the latter came close to war with France and Spain over a dispute with Spain over the control of the coast of what is now British Columbia. In 1790s, there were colonial disputes between Britain and Portugal, notably over the coastline north of Angola, and the latter was in the same position as Spain over Nootka Sound, as her own colonial position was based in part on historic claims to tracts of unoccupied territory; unoccupied by Europeans, that is, which was the issue in European diplomacy. It is not surprising that Portugal was not interested in the British idea that Lisbon serve as a naval base against Spain during the Nootka Sound Crisis.

In 1792, Portugal, like Britain, Spain and the Netherlands, did not go to war with Revolutionary France as Austria and Prussia did. However, in May 1792, Thomas Walpole, the envoy, reported:

A considerable number of French pamphlets and copies of the French constitution have arrived in one of the ports of this country. A spirit very much in opposition to the accustomed spirit of education in this country in theology, as well as politics, has been discovered among some of the students at the University of Coimbra; and although the government here was disposed not to take notice of what was at first represented as childish acts of impudence; it having since appeared that some chapels had been stripped of their ornaments and images; the offenders are said to have been brought down to Lisbon.

Already, radicalism had led to (unsuccessful) republican plots in Goa and Minas Gerais in 1787 and 1789 respectively. However, the key political problem in 1792 was that of responding to Maria's collapse into serious mental illness. John took over the government, albeit with some reluctance.

As Britain, faced with French threats to the Dutch, moved toward war with France in the winter of 1792–3, it pressed Portugal to arm. The Portuguese government was informed by the British that the Revolutionaries sought to overturn 'all existing governments ... carrying their principles into all the different countries of Europe'.

Portugal moved into the maelstrom with Britain, Spain and the Dutch in 1793, prefiguring the move to join the Allies during the First World War. Six thousand Portuguese troops were deployed alongside the Spaniards in the Pyrenees in 1793, but the French won there in 1794, and Spain abandoned the war in 1795 and, instead, allied with France. In response, Portugal became neutral, but that was an unstable position in the opportunistic international relations of the period. This was not least the case because putting pressure on Portugal was seen as a way of hitting at Britain, the policy already attempted in 1762.

Having gained power in France in late 1799, Napoleon pressed Spain to force Portugal to break with Britain. In 1800, John, who had formally become regent the previous year, refused and, in 1801, Spain and France invaded. This led to the 'War of the Oranges', a brief conflict. The Spanish force focused on a border conflict. They captured poorly defended Portuguese posts, notably Olivenza, but, when they attacked Elvas the assault was repulsed. The Spanish first minister, Manuel de Godoy, did not advance further into Portugal, despite picking oranges near Elvas and sending them to the Queen of Spain with the message that he would move on to Lisbon.

Begun on 20 May, the war ended on 6 June when Portugal agreed, by the Treaty of Badajoz, to cede Olivenza to Spain, pay a heavy indemnity and close its ports to British ships. In response, the British occupied Madeira in order to thwart a possible French or Spanish occupation of an island on key trade routes. In mainland Portugal, the fortress at Castelo Rodrigo, destroyed by the Spaniards as they evacuated it at the end of the war, remains in ruins. The issue of Olivenza continues to be contentious, with Portugal claiming that the invasion of 1807 made the Treaty of Badajoz invalid. Moreover, the Vienna Peace Treaty of 1815, which Spain signed in 1817, called for the return of Olivenza. However, it did so without effect.

Despite other European powers, notably Austria and Russia, turning against Napoleon in 1805 in the War of the Third Coalition, Portugal remained neutral until 1807, its ministers divided over whether to turn to Britain, to France or to remain neutral. The choice for the last was the easiest, as it left options, notably if Napoleon was defeated in Europe. However, he defeated Austria and Prussia and pushed Russia to terms, closing Europe to British trade. As a key part of this policy, Napoleon demanded that Portugal close its ports to British trade and when John, fearful for his empire, delayed, France and Spain invaded Portugal. John decided to close the ports, but too late.

A Lady of Note

Elizabeth, Lady Craven (1750–1828), the daughter of the Earl of Berkeley, was notorious for her scandalous personal life and for her travels. She married Charles Alexander, Margrave of Brandenburg-Ansbach, in Lisbon in September 1791, soon after the death of his first wife and her first husband. In her *Memoirs* she noted: 'The climate of Lisbon made my hair grow very long and extremely thick; and the salubrity of the air refreshed and invigorated my constitution.' Like other British commentators, including most of the accounts from soldiers who served in Portugal in 1808–13, she criticised the Portuguese for superstition and for their governmental system. Craven also disliked Portuguese bullfights, found Mafra 'a mixture of superstition and profusion', thought Sintra 'one of the most delicious spots in Europe' and wrote of the women:

> The Portuguese ladies are small in stature – their complexion is olive – their eyes generally black and expressive: they are both modest and witty, and are esteemed generous. Magnificent in their dress, but awkward in their manners, they keep their servants at a great distance, and expect a homage which is, perhaps, only due to royal personages. The furniture of their houses is grand beyond conception, and they maintain an immense number of domestics, as they never discharge any who have served them or their ancestors with fidelity.

9. The Crises of 1807–26

The French invasion in October 1807 under Jean-Andoche Junot culminated with the occupation of Lisbon on 30 November, after which he became Governor of Portugal. Unlike with the Spanish invasions of 1580 and 1762, there had been no resistance. However, Junot had found the advance overland from Salamanca difficult. The British had sent a fleet instructed to escort John, the regent on behalf of Maria I, to Brazil or to attack Lisbon if the government surrendered to the French. Under pressure from both sides, John finally decided to accept British protection, and he and a large entourage of about 15,000 people left for Brazil, much to the surprise of the public. The confused Maria was not sure where she was going. Although the lengthy journey in this case was far more arduous, this was on the pattern of the flight of several other rulers, those of Naples and Savoy-Piedmont to Sicily and Sardinia respectively under the cover of the British fleet, and Louis XVIII of France and William V of Orange to Britain. Delayed by contrary winds, John was unable to sail until the advancing French troops were on the very outskirts of the city. The plan itself was old. António Vieira had proposed it to John IV in the 1640s because of the Spanish threat. Brazil was the most valuable part of the Portuguese Atlantic empire.

The conquest of Portugal was intended by Napoleon to cement the 1806 Berlin and Milan Decrees that sought to establish the commercial quarantine of Britain and her goods, and thus weaken her economy and war effort. However, Napoleon's attempt to place his brother Joseph on the throne of Spain, a misconceived move that would have increased French control over Spanish resources, led to a popular uprising in Spain in 1808. The British exploited the situation with an expedition under Lieutenant-General Sir Arthur Wellesley, later Duke of Wellington, that landed in Portugal at Mondego Bay over the course of 1–5 August.

On 21 August 1808, this army defeated attacking French forces under Junot at Vimeiro. Wellesley had sheltered his lines of infantry from the French cannon by deploying them behind the crest of the ridge. He placed his riflemen forward in open order down the slope and used them to prevent the French skirmishers who advanced before the columns from disrupting the British lines. The poorly coordinated advancing columns were halted by British infantry and cannon fire, and driven back by downhill charges.

Wellesley was then superseded by superior officers, who did not wish to push on against the French. By the Convention of Sintra on 30 August, they agreed with the French that the latter evacuate Portugal, but be returned to France in British ships and be then free to resume hostilities. The British also agreed to ship the French baggage and booty. This agreement led to a public storm in Britain and the commanders were recalled to face a court of enquiry in London. Instead, Sir John Moore became the commander.

Napoleon, meanwhile, responded to the crisis in Spain by intervening in person, entering Madrid on 4 December 1808. Instructed to provide support for his Spanish opponents, Moore advanced into Spain from Lisbon, only, in the face of larger advancing French forces, to have to retreat, eventually to Corunna, from which the British troops could be shipped to Britain. Napoleon's plan for an advance on Lisbon had been thrown into disarray, but, having pursued Moore to Corunna, from which the British were evacuated, Marshal Jean-de-Dieu 'Nicolas' Soult then moved south to destroy the British forces in Portugal. These forces were garrisoning Lisbon under Lieutenant-General Sir John Francis Cradock. A cautious commander, and understandably so in the aftermath of Moore's failure, he felt that evacuation might be necessary.

The usually vigorous Soult stormed Oporto on 27 March 1809, but fresh British troops under Wellesley were sent to Portugal and he assumed command of the British army there. On 12 May, Wellesley made a surprise crossing of the Douro, fought off counterattacks and captured Oporto. This is a triumph that is commemorated in the city by the statue of a lion crushing an eagle. This was a well-executed offensive action that was helped by poor dispositions and slow responses on the part of Soult, who had wrongly thought he had seized all the boats that could be used for a crossing. Soult's force then retreated north-east, plundering and causing devastation, for example burning down much of the town of Amarante where the townspeople had defended the bridge when the French searched for a river crossing. From this devastation, the burned out ruins of an old manor house can be seen close to the railway station. Such destruction was commonplace with French campaigning and helps explain why recent attempts to praise Napoleon are seriously misplaced.

Another British force had been deployed to block a French advance on Lisbon from the east along the Tagus. However, the French, under Marshal Victor (Claude Victor-Perrin), short of food near Alcântara, halted their advance before they could reach the British force after the news of Wellesley's victory at Oporto. Indeed, it was the British that had wrecked the inflexible French strategy, one also hit by poor logistics. In general, the French assumed that they could seize the supplies they required, a practice that was militarily rash and politically inopportune, as well as being destructive.

In the winter of 1809–10, the end of war with Austria, the War of the Fourth Coalition, led to the dispatch of French reinforcements to Iberia, although France initially concentrated on its Spanish opponents. Given command of the Army of Portugal, a post he tried to refuse, Marshal André Masséna was then ordered to conquer that country. The threat of French attack led Wellesley, who had been elevated to the peerage as Viscount Wellington in August 1809, to fall back in 1810, avoiding battle with the far larger French army. His strategy was one of defence in depth, and he was given added time when Napoleon ordered Masséna, against the wishes of the latter who wanted to march direct on Lisbon, first to capture the strong border fortresses of Ciudad Rodrigo in Spain and Almeida in Portugal. Both fell, the second after the powder magazine was blown up on 27 August; but the sieges delayed Masséna. The envious Napoleon also provided Masséna with far fewer troops than he had promised.

Rather than withdrawing to Britain by sea, Wellington was convinced that Portugal could be held, and developed a strong fall-back fortified position – two lines of forts and natural obstacles, the Lines of Torres Vedras, resting on major water lines – to cover nearby Lisbon from the north. Despite the covering embrace of vegetation, it is still possible to follow important parts of these defences, notably the redoubts of São Vicente. There was a third line, protecting the fortress of São Julião da Barra, on the shore of the Tagus west of Lisbon, in case the British needed to protect a rushed evacuation.

Portugal was invaded by Masséna's army on 15 September. Wellington chose to resist Masséna's advancing forces further forward in a good defensive position at Buçaco on 27 September 1810. The French found the British and Portuguese drawn up on a ridge, and their poorly planned attacks were repulsed with nearly 5000 casualties, half of them Portuguese. A monument marks the victory, the Buçaco Palace Hotel has tiles depicting the battle, and there is a military museum nearby devoted to the war.

However, the position was then out-flanked, and Wellington fell back on the Lines of Torres Vedras. The French reached the Lines on 12 October, but they were too strong to breach, the French lacked a siege train and sufficient troops, and the devastated countryside meant that the French came to suffer serious malnutrition, just as the Spaniards had done when they invaded in 1762. Thanks to scorched-earth policies, Captain John Hill, a British soldier, recorded: 'The country is dreadfully ravaged. I saw nothing except a few pigeons left about the villages; the floors and rafters taken out either to burn or make huts. All the inhabitants had retired before our army, so that what a few months before had been a fine country is literally now a desert.'

Wellington focused on strengthening his position, denying Masséna the opportunity to fight a battle. Probing French moves failed. Napoleon thought that the British navy did not have the capacity to supply the million people within the Lines, but he was wrong. Napoleon, however, was happy to see British forces tied down in Lisbon and also thought that the Prince Regent might give up the struggle. The British officers, such as Wellington's second-in-command, Major-General Sir Brent Spencer, who doubted the viability of Wellington's plan of defence, were also wrong. Wellington had a mastery of logistics.

The winter did its damage, not least by greatly exacerbating French supply difficulties and, on 5 March 1811, after very heavy losses to disease and hunger, Masséna began to retreat. What in effect had been a large-scale siege of Lisbon by land had failed.

Masséna was followed by Wellington, who launched harassing attacks. To the north, Almeida was besieged by the British, and Masséna's attempt to relieve it were successfully blocked at Fuentes de Oñoro in early May. Almeida then fell. It remains an interesting fortress site with interpretation helped by a museum. Masséna was dismissed by a typically unforgiving Napoleon.

In 1811, 1812 and 1813, Wellington invaded Spain, with the Portuguese providing an important part of his manpower. A British officer, William Beresford, who had occupied Madeira in 1807, had been given supreme command of the Portuguese army in March 1809, and he totally reorganised it on British lines. Wellington had turned down the role. The Portuguese repeatedly fought hard, as at Buçaco (1810) and Albuera (1811), and, in the battle of Salamanca in 1812, a key victory, one third of the Allied casualties were Portuguese. They also fought well at the crucial battle of Vitoria, another key victory, in 1813. These Portuguese forces accompanied Wellington on his invasion of France in 1814. Wellington regarded them as better soldiers than the Spaniards and as better disciplined.

The war, however, left much of Portugal devastated and with heavy civilian casualties. The French invaders had inflicted much damage. Many civilians died as a result of their exactions, which included a massacre when Beja was sacked in 1808. There was also damage to monuments. Thus, in the monastery of Alcobaça, the tombs of Peter and Inês were damaged in 1811 by French troops seeking booty. In addition, agriculture had been badly hit during the war, which caused hunger. Moreover, trade was very much affected by British competition. Indeed, British economic and political influence was greatly resented, as was the army being under Beresford.

Political disaffection came to the fore on the death of Maria, when John VI came to the throne in March 1816. Aware of his wealth and position in Brazil, and not keen on another Atlantic crossing, he remained in Brazil. A regency was established in Portugal, and the army was still under Beresford. As with the Carnation Revolution in 1974, disaffection in the army was crucial in what became a revolutionary situation. In opposition, liberal agitation focused on the idea of calling a *cortes*, which had not met since 1698. Unlike with parliament in Britain, the government, thanks to Brazilian gold, had not needed to call a *cortes*. This agitation and the turn to a *cortes* were encouraged by the example of liberalism in Spain. In 1817, a group of revolutionaries under Gomes Freire de Andrade (who had served under Napoleon) was betrayed and executed.

This unpopular step contributed to the liberal revolution of 1820, which, on the pattern of Spanish developments, broke out in Oporto on 24 August, rapidly spreading elsewhere. The revolutionaries, who were opposed to the continued influence of Beresford, called for the return of John from Brazil, for a constitutional monarchy with a *cortes* modelled on the Spanish constitution of 1812, and for the reduction of Brazil from the status of a kingdom within the 'United Kingdom of Portugal, Brazil and the Algarve', a status granted by John in December 1815, to that of a colony. Without consulting John, they formed a government and called a *cortes* that met in 1821. This led to a Council of Regency to exercise power in the name of John. Political prisoners were freed, and John was pressed to return to Portugal. In accordance with the liberal agenda, the Inquisition was abolished in 1821 and religious orders were banned. Censorship was also banned until 1823 when the first law establishing the freedom of the press was passed.

In response, the indecisive John returned to Portugal in July 1821, leaving his talented son Peter as Regent of Brazil, and the constitution was approved in 1822. However, this revolution and the policies of the *cortes* were unpopular in Brazil, which, in turn, declared its independence on 7 September 1822, Peter becoming the first Emperor of Brazil. A war against the Portuguese forces in Brazil began in 1822 and lasted until 1824. The Portuguese forces were in the northern provinces and in the capital cities south of Rio. British naval officers and seamen recruited by Brazil played a key role in isolating Portuguese garrisons and enabling Brazil to win the war. In 1823, the Portuguese were forced to leave Salvador da Bahia, and the Brazilian squadron also captured Maranhão and Belém do Pará. Portugal was obliged to recognise Brazil's independence in 1825, with a British diplomat, Charles Stuart, playing a key role.

Brazilian independence was not inevitable, but highly contingent. Revolts in Brazil were spreading while the collapse of

Spanish America was an important background. The conflict in Brazil between the supporters of Portuguese rule and opponents was shorter than that in some parts of Spanish America, notably what became Venezuela, let alone in Spanish America as a whole, but was longer than in some other parts. As with Spain and the policies of the *cortes* there, the shifts in Portugal's policy affected the situation in Brazil.

In the outcome, many of the connections in the Luso-Atlantic world (Luso-, meaning 'related to Portugal', derives from the name of the Roman province Lusitania), notably those between Angola and Brazil, remained strong. However, the Portuguese world had been radically transformed by the loss of Brazil.

The last years of John VI's reign saw not only the loss of Brazil but also growing instability in Portugal, although nothing to match Spain, which faced civil war and French invasion in 1823. That year, opposition to liberalism began in Portugal, with a key role being played by John's second son, Prince Miguel, the 'Absolutist' or the 'Traditionalist'. He was encouraged by his Spanish mother, Queen Carlota Joaquina, long a political opponent of John's, as well as being an unfaithful wife. Miguel organised a military demonstration, the *Vilafrancada*, and forced forward the restitution of what he presented as his father's inalienable rights, that is, absolutist rights. In response to this pressure, John, who was personally sympathetic to liberalism, suspended the 1822 constitution and, under pressure, agreed to accept absolutism. However, the relationship with Miguel broke down in 1824. Backed by the British and French envoys, John then regained power in May and exiled Miguel. John, in turn, promised and did sketch, around 1825, a Constitutional Charter that would eventually assure a transition into a moderate liberalism, one separate from the *Vintismo* of the 1820 liberal revolution, and perhaps mirroring the Louis XVIII monarchy in France.

A Visitor in 1821–3

Having accompanied her husband, Alexander, to Portugal, Marianne Baillie published her account in 1824. Her impression was mixed. Staying in the outskirts of Lisbon, she complained of filth and bad smells in the streets, and the indolence of the inhabitants, adding: 'You are suffocated by the steams of fried fish, rancid oil, garlic etc at every turn, mingled with the foetid effluvia of decayed vegetables, stale provisions, and other horrors . . . the armies of fleas, bugs, mosquitos, and other vermin, are too numerous to be conceived even in idea.' She was more positive about Portuguese courtesy, roasted chestnuts and 'a sort of white light wine, sold here, which we thought almost as refreshing and as excellent as hock'.

Having recognised Brazilian independence, John restored the right of succession of his son Peter, the Emperor of Brazil, and also named a regency council under his daughter, the Infanta Isabel Maria, to govern the country between his death and the return of Peter. This offered the prospect of restoring the link between Portugal and Brazil, albeit as a dual monarchy. When John died, on 10 March 1826, a course for the stable future appeared set. It was not to be.

10. The Nineteenth-Century Monarchy, 1826–1910

On John VI's death, on 10 March 1826, his son, Peter, Emperor of Brazil and now Peter IV of Portugal, issued the Constitutional Charter in order to try to lessen the tension between liberals and absolutists. He also abdicated in favour of his daughter Maria, who was then seven, with the condition that she marry her uncle, Miguel. She became Maria II. Peter abdicated because he was aware that neither the Portuguese nor the Brazilians wanted a united kingdom.

Peter's brother, Miguel, returned from exile in Vienna as regent and fiancé of his niece, Maria. He argued that Peter had forfeited his claim to the Portuguese throne by declaring Brazilian independence. Isabel Maria, John's unmarried daughter, was regent from 1826 until 1828 when a civil war began: Miguel replaced Maria II (whom he never married), was proclaimed king by the *cortes*, and abolished the 1826 constitution. This led to the outbreak of fighting, with the garrison in Oporto declaring its loyalty to Peter IV, his daughter Maria and the Constitutional Charter. The rebellion, the opening stage in the Liberal Wars between the liberals and the absolutist, Miguelist faction, spread, but was brutally suppressed by Miguel who was backed by the Church and the landowners, both of whom were concerned by liberalism. Many liberals fled abroad, to Spain or Britain. Others were arrested. Isabel Maria had retired from politics and turned to piety.

In 1831, Peter abdicated in Brazil in favour of his son and sailed for Europe to challenge Miguel. This took much effort and many years, and the accompanying conflict and disruption inflicted much economic damage, damage that plays a role in helping explain the low economic growth rate of the period. Peter first established a government in liberal-run Terceira in the Azores.

The following July, Peter landed near Oporto which he captured, only to be besieged there. On 5 July 1833, however, Miguel's fleet was beaten by the smaller liberal navy under Sir Charles Napier off Cape St Vincent, after landing an expedition under a leading liberal, the Duke of Terceira, in the Algarve. The naval battle was settled in hand-to-hand fighting.

From the Algarve, Terceira marched north through the Alentejo, defeating the Miguelists on 23 July at Almada/Cova da Piedade, after which the liberals occupied Lisbon. Miguelist attempts to storm Oporto and Lisbon were repulsed with heavy losses. Maria was proclaimed queen anew in 1833 and Peter made regent. He confiscated the property of Miguel's supporters and suppressed the monasteries.

In 1834, Terceira and the Duke of Saldanha defeated the Miguelists at Almoster (18 February) and Asseiceira (16 May). The last, fought near Tomar, was decisive, with the Miguelists suffering heavy casualties. Eight days later, faced by disaffection from his officers, Miguel surrendered at Évora. By the subsequent Concession of Évoramonte on 26 May, he surrendered his claim to the throne and was banished. Peter died soon after, on 24 September 1834, his legacy including an equestrian statue in *Liberdade* square in Oporto.

Both sides had been very short of funds and, compared to the campaigning in Portugal during the Peninsular War, this conflict was under resourced. The manpower, materiel and funds that the British and French had been able to provide during the Peninsular War were all lacking. Nevertheless, that did not mean that military skill was absent, as Saldanha showed in 1834. The civil war was destructive, including deliberate devastation, as with the burning of the town of Albufeira by Miguel's supporters in

1833. This civil war was the most destructive conflict in post-Napoleonic Portuguese history, although comparisons with the colonial wars of the 1960s and early 1970s are difficult.

Civil war did not help Portugal's overseas position either. It was no longer able to maintain a successful imperial impetus. In Mozambique, the Zulu, an expansionist people, sacked Lourenço Marques in 1833. In Angola, the Portuguese moved into the central plateau in the mid-1830s and established a fort at São Salvador in the mid-1850s, but it was abandoned in 1866.

Although Miguel, once in exile, denounced the Concession, the Miguelists did not have the persistence in Spain of the Carlists, another counter-revolutionary movement that also drew on peasant anger against government. However, instability continued. In September 1836, the radicals seized power in Portugal, the same year in which there was a successful liberal revolution in Spain. In both countries, the politicisation of the army was a key factor. It was the principal body that could stage and/or resist coups or rebellions, a situation that looked toward its crucial role in Portugal and Spain in the twentieth century.

Saldanha benefited from his success in 1834 in serving as president of the Council in 1835. In 1836, however, the situation went out of control, with a revolt by officers in August followed by a revolution in September and the reinstating of the 1822 constitution by the *Setembristas*. Maria fled to Belém and sought to sponsor a counter-revolution, but, in the face of threats from the *Setembristas*, she failed. In turn, in 1837, in the Revolt of the Marshals, Saldanha and Terceira, with British backing, tried, and failed, to overthrow the new government. The *Setembristas* then organised a militant National Guard that dominated Lisbon, only to be suppressed by troops in March 1838.

Fresh insurrections followed in 1842 and 1844. Saldanha became president of the Council in 1846–9, 1851–6 and 1870, the last a military dictatorship. A revolutionary insurrection in the Minho in the spring of 1846 which, in October, became a civil war known as the Patuleia or Little Civil War, was crushed by royalist troops that December in the battle of Torres Vedras. This instability was scarcely unique in Europe, but it helped explain the problems facing economic growth.

The inexperienced Maria II (r. 1826–8, 1834–53) had two husbands. Her first husband, Auguste, Duke of Leuchtenberg, died two months after the marriage, but, in 1836, she married Prince Ferdinand of Saxe-Coburg-Gotha, a marriage that lasted. The cousin of the Prince Albert who married Queen Victoria of Britain, he was a keen patron of the arts, and built an extravagant summer palace at Pena near Sintra. Maria sought to improve educational provision and to tackle cholera. The *Teatro Nacional de Dona Maria II*, built in Lisbon in the 1840s, is a lasting monument to the reign. Maria's government was opposed by left-wing liberals seeking to curb royal authority on the lines of the constitution of 1822. Her supporters were the *Cartistas*, upholding the Constitutional Charter of 1826 granted by her father, Peter IV. There were calls for modernisation and socio-economic improvement, notably from Mouzinho da Silveira. Maria died, aged only thirty-four, in 1853. Obesity and difficult pregnancies were the causes of this early death.

Maria's son, Peter V (r. 1853–61), who started reigning at the age of eighteen in 1855 after a two-year regency period under his father, Don Fernando, pursued policies of modernisation, notably in infrastructure and public health. Railways and roads were constructed in a period that lasted into the next reign and was called the Regeneration. Peter pleased Victoria when he visited her in Britain because, although he went to Mass, he criticised the ignorance and immorality of Portuguese society and praised his host country.

However, with two of his brothers, Peter fell victim to an epidemic and, as a result of a childless marriage, was succeeded by his brother Luís I (r. 1861–89). Luís's legacy included the palace of Ajuda in Belém, an expensive Neoclassical work, and he was also responsible for the development of Cascais as a summer resort. As with Italy and Spain, government alternated between two groupings, one of which was more conservative and less liberal than the others. In Portugal, this meant the *Regeneradores* and the *Progressistas*, in a pattern of frequent and destabilising changes known as the *Rotativism*. The King favoured the former, backing their dominance of the 1880s. By British standards, the Conservative Party (*Regeneradores*) was not illiberal and its liberal rival not particularly popular. The illiberals were only the remaining Miguelists.

Luís's son, Charles I (r. 1889–1908), faced more difficult domestic circumstances with an increase in both republicanism and radicalism, which was part of a European pattern. In 1900, Charles responded to republican electoral success in Oporto by quashing the result (which led to the election of new republicans), and ended the session of the *cortes* in order to quieten republicanism there. The political system no longer appeared to be delivering acceptable results or certainly those that offered a consensus.

The King responded, in May 1907, by imposing a dictatorial-style government under João Franco, who got Charles to dismiss parliament when he lost his majority without an immediate call for elections. Charles granted that, conceding to Franco what he had denied a year earlier to Ernesto Hintze Ribeiro, the leader of the Regenerator Party who had been prime minister in 1893–7, 1900–4 and 1906. The government was called by then an 'administrative dictatorship'. Franco, who had come to power in May 1906 with the support of the King, sought a government of popularity and order, one in which royalism was to be defended in a strong fashion while the traditional élites were bypassed in a search for popular backing. Initially successful, this policy ran adrift of the constitutional limitations on government. In response, Franco became increasingly authoritarian, not least with a vigorous censorship of the press. However, this stance compromised the popularity of both government and monarchy. Charles was assassinated by two anarchists in the *Terreiro do Paço* in central Lisbon on 1 February 1908. His wounded eldest son, Luís Felipe, was also killed after shooting back from the royal carriage.

The money spent by the kings on palaces, for example the Neo-Manueline one at Buçaco built on the site of a Carmelite monastery, commissioned as a hunting lodge by Charles in 1888 and finished in 1907, was a marked contrast to the poverty of most of their subjects. The republicans attacked royal expenditure, which was a key political issue, and notably so as in 1907 when Franco increased the government grant to the Crown and paid off the Crown's debts.

Charles's younger son, who became Manuel II in 1908, only ruled until 1910. Charles's murder was followed by the dismissal on 4 February of Franco, the murderers' initial target, and he went into exile. Manuel, however, did not benefit from any surge in popularity, although he tried to win support by ending press censorship and releasing those imprisoned under Franco for political beliefs. The recent increase in the grant to the Crown was reversed, and some palaces became national monuments, including Sintra, Ajuda and Queluz.

Nevertheless, governmental stability could not be gained, in part because the republicans wanted the overthrow of the monarchy. In Manuel's brief reign alone, there were six ministries. In 1910, in the context of growing ministerial instability, and of a steadily more militant Republican Party, he was overthrown in a republican revolution that broke out on 3 October. Troops set up barricades in Lisbon, and the royal palace was shelled by two warships. This was a military coup backed by the *Carbonária*, a secret republican organisation. There was some opposition from within the army, which led to fighting, and only limited public support for the revolution, but republicanism had backing in the middle class and had triumphed in the municipal elections in

Lisbon in 1908. As in Brazil in 1889, the military played the key role in 1910.

On 5 October 1910, faced by the republican takeover in Lisbon, Manuel sailed from Ericeira, not to Oporto to call for support, as he may have sought, but, instead, for exile in Britain. There, he lived in Fulwell Park, Twickenham, until he died in 1932. Manuel's bedroom can be seen in the Pena Palace in the *Serra de Sintra*. Three years earlier, Franco had died, but back in Portugal.

Empire

With the loss of Brazil, Portugal had lost an empire, but failed to gain a role. Portugal, meanwhile, had seen imperial expansion, although not on the scale of Britain, France, the Netherlands or Germany. Control over Angola and Mozambique increased in the 1890s, in part because there was no disaster to match that which faced Italy at Ethiopian hands at Adua in 1896; and these successes left the memorabilia preserved in military museums, such as those in Bragança and Lisbon. The ability to win local support was important to Portuguese success. To a degree, this ability was a product of local rivalries. Thus, in defeating the kingdom of Gaza in Mozambique in 1895, the squares of Portuguese infantry used their Kropatschek magazine rifles to defeat Gaza charges, but the Portuguese also benefited from rebellions against the kingdom by its subject people. In the Zambezi Valley, the Portuguese took over the strongholds of warlords they defeated and in some cases occupied them with garrisons. The fortified post, sometimes called a *presidio*, was the nucleus for a rudimentary administration. For the most part, the soldiers who garrisoned them were *'cipais'*, African soldiers fighting for Portugal. New Portuguese forts in the colonies were square in shape with corner turrets and sometimes with strengthened bastions for mounting artillery.

North of the River Congo, Portugal established Cabinda as a protectorate in 1885, although the great powers meeting in the Conference of Berlin that year, by extending the Congo Free State's boundary to the sea, ensured that Angola and Cabinda were not territorially joined. Portugal's position there was consolidated by 1901. There was also expansion into the interior from Portuguese Guinea, but, as with the British colony of Gambia, this was small-scale due to a much greater and all-encompassing expansion of the French in the region. So also to the south of Lourenço Marques in Mozambique, with small successive advances in 1875 and 1891, but British expansion northward into Zululand from Natal was extensive and blocked Portuguese opportunities.

Expansion in Africa, notably the *contra-costa* plan to link Angola and Mozambique through the establishment of intervening colonies, was seen, particularly by the Lisbon Geographical Society founded in 1875, as a way of reviving Portugal's strength and fulfilling its imperial destiny, replacing long-lost Brazil. This was similar to Britain making extensive Indian gains soon after the loss in 1783 of the Thirteen Colonies of what became the United States. The coast-to-coast Portuguese advance in Africa appeared viable for most of the nineteenth century. In 1880, the lands in between Angola and Mozambique were occupied by native territories, principally Lunda, the Kololo Empire and the Matabele Empire. This remained the case in the mid-1880s. There were now German colonies, in East Africa (now Tanzania) and South-West Africa (Namibia), but the boundary lines recognised for them in 1886, although favourable to Germany, and for the free trade zone of the Congo Free State established by the Berlin Act of 1885 and run by Leopold II of Belgium, still left plenty of room for a coast-to-coast Portuguese empire.

However, the Berlin Conference also emphasised the need for establishing sufficient authority as the basis for advancing territorial claims. This provision led to Portuguese activity from 1884, including the establishment that year of the town of Beira, and, in 1889, the attempt to stake claims in modern Zimbabwe and Malawi. Portuguese hopes were thwarted by northward British expansion into what became Southern Rhodesia (Zimbabwe), Northern Rhodesia (Zambia) and Nyasaland (Malawi). In Britain, missionary supporters backing the Scottish missions in the Shire Highlands (Malawi) played a key role as did supporters of Cecil Rhodes's British South Africa Company. A British ultimatum in 1890, related to expansion from Mozambique, not Angola, and demanded the withdrawal of the Portuguese troops that had moved forward from Mozambique in 1888–9. This ultimatum resulted in treaties in 1891 and 1899 that stabilised Portugal's colonial boundaries, forcing Portugal to abandon its claims, based on historical discovery and recent exploration, as laid out in the Rose-Coloured Map of 1886 (an annex to a supposedly secret Portuguese-German convention signed in 1886), and leaving the lands in between open to British expansion. Portugal was obliged to accept British control of what became the Rhodesias and the British protectorate of what became Botswana. In 1905, the border between Angola and Northern Rhodesia was settled. Moreover, the Boer republics of the Orange Free State and the Transvaal were left more clearly in the British sphere of interest, and the Boer War of 1899–1902 established British control in both.

Under pressure, the ultimatum, which was seen as a national humiliation for Portugal, was accepted by Charles I and helped make the government and the King unpopular. Indeed, it led to anti-British rioting in Oporto in 1890, including the storming of the consul's house, and an attempted republican coup there in 1891. The Portuguese ministry fell in 1890 as a result of the terms of a draft treaty. Charles continued to be closely associated with Britain, which he visited anew in 1895, 1901, 1902 and 1904. He had received the Order of the Garter in 1891. However, the 1890 ultimatum began the instability of Portugal's 'long twentieth century' and, in particular, a series of dramatic political breaks. An idea of national failure gathered pace.

With a foreign debt of over £140 million in 1890, a serious balance of payments problem and falling gold reserves, Portugal, which declared a partial repudiation of its foreign debt in 1892, was in no state to resist. Indeed, in 1898, the Portuguese financial crisis resulted in a secret Anglo-German treaty allocating Angola and Mozambique in the event of Portugal wishing to sell them. France was also interested in Angola. There was no such sale but, instead, another fiscal crisis in 1902.

Separately, in 1904, Portugal agreed with the Dutch to divide the island of Timor. This was followed in 1912 by the Portuguese suppression of the independent Timorese nobles. However, whereas the Dutch had rapidly taken over what eventually became Indonesia, there was no Portuguese expansion in the region other than in what became East Timor.

Nineteenth-Century Changes

The nineteenth-century left impressive signs and symbols of change in metropolitan Portugal. In Oporto, more particularly, there is a series of bridges across the Douro. The first, a pontoon bridge, built in 1806, had collapsed under refugees fleeing French forces in 1809. From the 1840s on, a number of bridges survive in Oporto, most dramatically the 1877 Maria Pia Bridge, a wrought iron structure that was then the longest single-arch span in the world. Support from British merchants and a design by Gustave Eiffel were the key elements. Although no longer used, the bridge remains dramatic. It was followed by the double-deck Dom Luís I Bridge, designed by Théophile Seyrig, which, when opened in 1886, had the longest span of its type in the world. Metro trams now cross the bridge. Bridges and other works, such as the Glória (1885) and Santa Justa (1902) elevators in Lisbon, were dramatic signs of modernity.

So also was the endorsement of aspects of the liberal agenda. In 1842, an Anglo-Portuguese treaty abolished the slave trade. However, it proved difficult to stamp out the trade which provided the prime source of Brazil's slaves, not least because Portuguese officials in Angola colluded with it. In 1861, Charles Buxton MP complained to the British Prime Minister Viscount Palmerston, claiming that where was now 'scarcely any slave trade except from' Portugal's African colonies. Buxton suggested offering Portugal the assistance of two or three British consuls to watch the conduct of the officials, the sort of infringement of sovereignty that other powers found unacceptable. Portugal followed up by abolishing slavery in 1861.

There continued, however, to be multiple overlaps between servitude and the Portuguese world. Trying to make Angola a smaller version of Brazil, producing sugar and coffee for export, the Portuguese colonial government relied (illegally) on surreptitious slaving, but the policy failed. The Portuguese also sought to use indentured servants to grow cocoa on São Tomé.

The nationalisation of the lands of the monasteries in Portugal in 1834 was another major sign of modernity. This was a measure passed by the minister of justice, Joaquim António de Aguiar, a liberal. He went on to be prime minister in 1841–2, 1860 and 1865–8, and was referred to as the 'Killer of Friars' because of his action against the monasteries. As in England in the sixteenth century, monastic buildings and estates became a source of profit for others. Most of the land was purchased by existing landowners and by speculators. The extensive urban properties were used for the state, with the parliament, the *Palácio de São Bento*, housed in a former convent, for the army, for example the Santa Clara convent in Coimbra, by the police and by other state bodies. The measure was anti-clerical and directed at those associated with Miguel, rather than leading to social reform. This change to institutions that had been active for centuries was registered in the details of life across the country. Local patterns of social welfare were greatly affected. The measure did not increase popular support for the government or the political system.

Portugal abolished the death penalty in 1867 for all crimes except in the military (and for all crimes in 1911). This was far in advance of most states, although Venezuela had done so in 1863. Victor Hugo praised such a humanitarian country. The last execution in Portugal took place in 1846. The death penalty was subsequently reintroduced for military crimes in 1916, with one execution accordingly in 1917 (in France during the war), and was abolished anew in 1976.

A very different form of change was offered by the development of a railway system from 1856. That year, the first railway line, that from Lisbon to Carregado, was opened. A network spread, albeit far more slowly than in France or Britain. Lisbon was linked into the European system via the Portuguese rail junction of Entroncamento and via Badajoz in Spain. In 1887, a line along the Douro that had begun in 1875 was completed and, also that year, the *Sud Express* first ran from Paris to Lisbon via Madrid. In 1888, the service was run twice weekly from London, becoming a daily from 1907.

Townscapes were changed as stations were built and lines driven through. The stations were major works. Finished in 1887, Rossio station in Lisbon was built in a Neo-Manueline style with Moorish-style horseshoe arches. The original Oporto railway station was followed in 1903 by the more central São Bento train station, finished in 1916 on the site of a monastery. It was enhanced in 1930 by about 20,000 tiles that show the history of transport as well as historic battle scenes, including Henry the Navigator's conquest of Ceuta in 1415, and is a tourist site today. The development of a train system increased the need for coal, but Portugal had no production of coal or iron, which increased its dependence on Britain.

Charles Meyer's impressive 1844 map of Lisbon showed it before the impact of the railway. The city was spreading along the coast and inland, but it remained focused on Baixa and the hills on either side. The railway led to major changes. So also did urban development schemes that drew on greater prosperity and the need to support a growing city. The *Avenida da Liberdade* created in the 1880s was a central axis that shaped a northward spread of the city. In turn, that was taken onwards by the Rotunda, with its central statue of Pombal, and then by the *Parque Eduardo VII*; the King paid a state visit. Tourists included Alfred, Lord Tennyson who went from Lisbon to Sintra, which he surprisingly described as 'rather cockney'. There was new money, for example in the Lapa area of Lisbon.

So also with Oporto. Oporto's stock-exchange, built from 1842 to 1910 on the site of the monastery of St Francis, shows the wealth of the period. The introduction in Oporto in 1895 of the first electric trams in Iberia was a sign of innovation. Indeed, the tram museum in Oporto testifies to other aspects of the transformation of transport in the nineteenth century. Much of the investment necessary for economic development in Portugal came from abroad, notably Britain. This was the case for example of the port trade, of railways, of mineral deposits and of the empire as a whole. Portugal also played a key role in the British Empire, as in 1870 when a telegraph station was established in Carcavelos by the Falmouth, Malta and Gibraltar Co. (later Cable and Wireless), a part of a system linking Britain to India via the Mediterranean. The British staff fielded one of the cricket teams that reflected the range of British activity in the country. The station was sold in 1963.

Other aspects of British influence emerged in the life and writings of Júlio Dinis (1839–71), the pseudonym of Joaquim Guilherme Gomes Coelho, an Oporto doctor and writer who had a British mother, and, before dying of tuberculosis, published *Pupilas do Senhor Reitor* (*The Pupils of the Dean*, 1867) and *Uma Família Inglesa* (*An English Family*, 1868). These popular novels focused on anglophile middle-class life.

Eça de Queirós: Realist Writer

In the Chiado in Lisbon, the statue of José Maria de Eça de Queirós, erected by António Teixeira Lopes in 1903, has the famous novelist accompanied by the kind of female muse most writers can only dream about. An illegitimate child, born in Póvoa de Varzim in 1845, he studied in Coimbra and became a journalist, moving on to become a municipal administrator in Leiria and then a consul, serving in Newcastle, Bristol and Paris. Set in Leiria, his novel *O Crime do Padre Amaro* (*The Crime of Father Amaro*, 1875) deals with clerical affairs and infanticide. Filmed in 2005, this became the then most successful Portuguese film in box-office history. Another realist novel, *Os Maias* (1888), tackles the fictional Maias family as a way to consider Portugal's decline. Unwitting incest is a key element in the story.

A very different picture to the cities was offered by rural and small town Portugal. These areas saw scant economic development and, instead, grinding poverty and a pervasive conservatism. The global economic problems of the late nineteenth century played through particularly harshly in Portugal. Its agriculture suffered from the competition of New World grain and meat, with goods speeded to Europe by steamship, while industry and shipping was affected by foreign rivals. Tax revenues and employment were both hit hard.

Population pressures were a major issue. The violent disruption of the Peninsular War had led to a fall of Portugal's population to 2.9 million in 1811 but, thereafter, at a time of major expansion in the world's population, there was a steady rise, to 6 million by 1911. This rise was despite serious losses due to disease, particularly thanks to urban crowding and outbreaks of infectious diseases, notably cholera, as in 1833. Moreover, emigration took away part of the population growth, especially in the second half of the century, when there was large-scale movement to Brazil. As with Britain and the United States during this century, the key destination of emigrants was no longer a colony. It proved far harder to persuade people to emigrate to tropical lands.

The rise in the population pressed hard on living standards. It also led to significant movement within Portugal, especially to the cities, which became more crowded. This was a background to prolonged, and rising, social strain and political radicalism. At the same time, by the turn of the century, about 85 per cent of the population still lived in rural areas. The employment structure was 57 per cent agriculture, 21.5 per cent industry and 21.5 per cent services.

Independent Brazil

Just as Britain's history was to be affected by the role and impact of the United States once independent, so Brazil remained highly significant in the Portuguese world. This was particularly so as an alternative political model within this world; a destination for emigration from Portugal, a more attractive one than Portugal's African colonies; as a crucial economic link for the latter, notably Angola; and as important to the economy of mainland Portugal.

Unlike Spanish America, Portuguese America held together, which very much limited the potential options for continued Portuguese political influence there. Indeed, unlike Spain in the 1860s, Portugal was not to seek to intervene militarily in its former empire. There was a number of serious rebellions in Brazil: by the *Cabanos* in Pernambuco in 1832–5 and in Pará in 1835–6, the *Sabinada* in Bahia in 1837–8, the *Balaida* in Maranhão in 1839–40, and the *Farrapos* in Rio Grande do Sul and Santa

Catarina in 1835–45. Social tension played a major role in these risings, with popular opposition to social and economic dominance by the élite, especially by large landowners. Government forces were hindered by the size of the areas of operation, poor communications, and a lack of adequate training, pay and food, which led to desertion; and the situation was exacerbated by the disruption caused by the conflict. The political strains led to suspicion and divisions on the government side.

However, the rebellions all failed. In part, this was due to a lack of cooperation between the rebels, but other factors played a role. In the case of the *Cabanos*, guerrilla operations created grave difficulties for the government forces until, at the close of 1834, more active measures were put in place, especially maintaining the initiative, destroying *Cabano* crops in the forest regions, and hanging those thought to be *Cabanos*. The population suspected of sympathy for the rebels was removed, and the *Cabanos* were isolated and increasingly short of food. Desertion was encouraged, not least through the active use of the Church.

Brazil also acted as a major regional power in a way that Portugal could not do. It struggled with Argentina in 1825–30 in a conflict over control of Uruguay, which Brazil had annexed in 1816. In 1825, a Uruguay patriot, Juan Lavalleja, rebelled and, gaining support, defeated the Brazilians at Rincón de las Gallinas and Sarandí. Because Argentina accepted his proposal for union, this became a full-scale war, in which southern Brazil was invaded in 1829. The more powerful Brazilian navy blockaded Buenos Aires. Neither side was able to gain a decisive advantage, but the Brazilians held on to their major positions in Uruguay throughout the war. The peace settlement left Uruguay independent as a buffer state.

In the War of the Triple Alliance of 1864–70, Brazilian military intervention led to the liberals gaining power in Uruguay in 1864. This was opposed by the egotistical Paraguayan president, Marshal Francisco López, an opponent of Brazilian expansion, and he invaded Brazil in 1865. Brazil bore the bulk of the alliance effort against Paraguay and provided the army of occupation after López's death in 1870.

Meanwhile, under British pressure Brazil had ended its import of slaves in 1850, to all intents and purposes. Slavery was increasingly regarded in influential circles, especially in the expanding cities, as a cause of unrest and a source of national embarrassment and relative backwardness. It was abolished in the Portuguese Empire in 1861. As part of the process by which New World settler societies were culturally dependent on the Old World, the Brazilian élite looked to Europe to validate their sense of progress. Moreover, the combination of the end of the slave trade with economic expansion meant that slavery was no longer able to supply Brazil's labour needs. A growing need for artisans, furthermore, could not be met from the traditional Brazilian slave economy.

As free labour became more important, slave-owners were increasingly isolated. In 1884, two provinces freed their slaves, while increased numbers of slaves fled, so that by 1887 only about 5 per cent of the population remained as slaves. There was considerable support for slave flight, with much of the populace as well as the bulk of the authorities, including the army, unwilling to support the owners. This contrasted with the earlier situation in the American South. Whereas in the latter, the stress was on regarding white society as the people, in Brazil the emphasis was on a multicultural society. The 1888 Golden Law, passed by an overwhelming majority in parliament, freed the remaining slaves and without compensation for the owners. This hit the sugar economy of the north-east and was a key aspect of a more general agrarian depression that affected the old order in Brazil, weakening the imperial monarchy. In a related, but important, rejection of the past, Brazil became a republic in 1889. Portugal followed twenty-one years later.

11. Republican Instability and Salazarist Autocracy, 1910–74

Republican Instability

The republican revolution in 1910 was followed by instability and frequent changes in government. There were changes in symbolism, from the national anthem to place names. Thus, in Lisbon in 1910, the name of the *Rua das Trinas* was changed to *Rua Sara de Matos*, whom it was alleged had been murdered by nuns, and a large monument was built to this 'martyr' at the Prazeres Cemetery. Across the country, the main town square became the *Praça da República*. In place of the former national flag, which had been the royal arms over a blue-and-white rectangle, a new flag, adopted in 1911, adopted red and green, the colours of the Republican Party, with the national coat of arms over the colour boundary.

Church and state were formally separated during the republic. All the religious orders were abolished, Church properties were seized and education secularised, while action was taken against popular religious festivals. Divorce was legalised and in 1911 widows were given the vote as heads of families, although in 1913 they were excluded from that right. Women did not get the right to vote on an equal footing until the 1976 constitution. Palaces became national monuments. The royal palace in Lisbon was turned into government offices. The murderers of the King and Crown Prince in 1908 were rehabilitated.

Political instability was acute. There was monarchist pressure, notably incursions of monarchists from Spain near Chaves in October 1911 and July 1912 that, however, were quickly driven back by Republican troops, as well as the proclamation of a Monarchy of the North in Oporto in January 1919. The latter, which was not backed by Manuel II, was rapidly suppressed.

More seriously, the Republican movement splintered badly, with many changes in government. In January 1915, in order to circumvent the *cortes* which was dominated by the Republicans, a conservative government was formed under General Joaquim Pimenta de Castro, a career military officer, but this was overthrown in May 1915 by military support for the Republicans.

The First World War

Adding to the political crisis was the outbreak of war in Europe in 1914. Like much of Europe that year, Portugal remained neutral, as Spain did throughout the war. At the same time, Portugal had to adapt to the possibility of war. The first civilian air club was established in 1909, but it was only the Republican regime that started to think about adding aircraft to the armed forces. In 1914, in parallel with the debate about entering the war, the government established what was called the Military Aeronautic Service and bought from France for the army the first military aircraft in Portugal.

Portugal long remained neutral, but its trade was hit by British and German economic warfare. Eventually, under British pressure focused on strengthening the blockade of Germany, Portugal entered the war in March 1916 on the Allied side. This unpopular and expensive decision was bitterly criticised by the trade unions. Portugal had interned German and Austrian ships in Lisbon the previous month in response to a British request. Germany declared war on 9 March. The government saw the war as the key to a glorious future for Portugal.

Troops were sent to the Western Front, arriving there in April 1917. There were heavy losses for the Portuguese troops there in the battle of the Lys on 9 April 1918 in the German Spring Offensives. The Portuguese Second Division held the centre of the attacked position and, poorly commanded and with variable morale, it was overrun with the loss of about 7400 men, mostly made prisoner. There had already been fighting with German troops in Africa from 1914.

The war also brought change to the military. Within the Portuguese Expeditionary Corps deployed to northern France in 1917, an air-combat unit was planned. It was not sent, but single officers with flying expertise were posted to British and French units and thus became the first Portuguese fighter pilots. Also in 1917, the navy established its Aviation Service and School, while, in Mozambique in 1917–18, there were Portuguese air operations against forces invading from neighbouring German East Africa.

Portugal mobilised 105,500 troops; 55,000 went to the Western Front, and the rest to Africa. The war cost about 7760 dead, 16,600 wounded, 13,600 missing in action and prisoners, and 96 ships sunk.

Instability, 1917–25

The unpopular, anti-clerical government of Afonso Costa, prime minister on three occasions, was overthrown in December 1917 by a Revolutionary Committee under Sidónio Pais, a prominent Republican and opponent of the war who benefited from popular anger with wartime shortages, although the coup essentially relied on only 250 men. This committee was referred to by its supporters as the New Republic. The confused nature of the confrontation in Lisbon was captured by Major-General Nathaniel Barnardiston, the Chief of the British Military Mission: 'the fleet got to work . . . and the field pieces replied but were almost all short. I only saw one go over and none apparently anywhere near . . . There was intermittent rifle fire all night as rioters were looting shops etc.' The Prime Minister was imprisoned and the President deposed.

Costa went into exile in Paris. The new dictatorship, with Pais as president, prime minister, war minister and minister of foreign affairs, continued Portugal's role in the war, and also responded within Portugal with force to conspiracies and riots, leading to a state of emergency in October 1918. However, Pais was assassinated that December in the main Lisbon railway station by a left-wing activist. The liberal republic returned, and gained the East African Kionga Triangle in the post-war Treaty of Versailles: the area had been seized by the Portuguese in 1916, rectifying a German encroachment on Portuguese territory in 1894.

Alongside a measure of modernism in Portuguese culture and society, for example the spread of the cinema, of aviation and of the press, political instability continued, as was also the case across much of Europe, including Spain. Indeed, modernism was a reaction to the perception that democracy had failed and that Portugal had become decadent. This was an aspect of the culture wars that was to be won by traditionalism.

At the same time, radicalism, authoritarianism and the varied types of Republican continuity, were all in a dynamic and destructive tension. The existing system was under much pressure. There were frequent strikes. The Republican government was unpopular due to anti-clericalism and economic instability. There were many changes in government, some due to force. Prime Minister António Granjo and two other key moderate Republican politicians were assassinated on 19 October 1921 during the Bloody Night, a radical revolt by junior officers.

In the end, the government of President Bernardino Machado was overthrown by an army coup in 1926 that created a conservative order. The coup of 28 May, moreover, ended the Portuguese First Republic. Much of the army had not forgiven the republic for sending it into the First World War. Two failed coups in 1925 had not ended military agitation against the republic, which was led, after the victory of the Republican Party in the elections of 8 November 1925, by António Maria da Silva.

The plotters in 1926 benefited from the support of General Manuel Gomes da Costa, who had commanded on the Western Front in 1918. He led the revolution in Braga and, from there, it rapidly spread on 29 May 1926 to Oporto, Lisbon and other major cities. The government resigned that day, and the coup leader in Lisbon, José Mendes Cabeçadas, a democratic sympathiser, became prime minister, with an economist, António de Oliveira Salazar, soon after made minister of finance.

Salazar in Power

A keen Catholic, Salazar was born in 1889 in Vimieiro to a family of small landowners. Educated for eight years at a seminary, Salazar eventually decided not to become a priest and, instead, studied law at the University of Coimbra, developing a particular interest in finance and economic policy. Becoming an academic at Coimbra, he was appalled by the political and economic instability of the First Republic, which he depicted as chaos, as well as horrified by its anti-clericalism. In 1933, he reflected on the situation prior to his regime: 'Our revolutions, our apparent incapacity to govern ourselves, the rottenness of our administration, our general backwardness, all were held up to our national discredit.'

In June 1926, after another coup, Gomes da Costa took power, only for him to be forced into exile the following month as a result of a coup by more conservative figures. Another general, António Óscar de Fragoso Carmona, then took power and survived two coup attempts that September. He was president from November 1926 to April 1951 when he died. Carmona reappointed Salazar minister of finance in 1928 and nominated him as prime minister in 1932. Oppressed by a heavy public debt, the new government faced bankruptcy, and this made Salazar, a monetarist who set out, by imposing austerity, to balance the budget, particularly influential. Carmona became a figurehead, and Salazar, who served as prime minister until 1968, was the key figure under the new constitution of 1933 that officially established the *Estado Novo* (New State), as the Second Republic was known.

Drawing on papal encyclicals of 1891 and 1931, this was a corporatist, authoritarian state pledged to national regeneration. Salazar was opposed to party government. A civilian regime, not a militarist one, the *Estado Novo* used troops, such as those deployed in 1934 against strikes, but relied more on the *Polícia de Vigilância e Defesa do Estado*, a highly effective secret police force established in 1933 that was ready to use brutal means. Towns were physically dominated by military garrisons and police stations, and the new fascist-style architecture was often that of control as in the courthouse in Oporto. The regime also had a uniformed paramilitary organisation (the Portuguese Legion) and youth movement.

Censorship also played an important role. It was both political and ideological in its character, and, more generally, opposed to new ideas, and thus modernism. The regime was clear in its hostility to communism, atheism, socialism, anarchism, democracy and liberalism. Freemasonry, which was closely linked to the Republican Party and was anti-clerical, was attacked under the new regime from 1929 and in 1935 it was declared illegal to be a Freemason. This legislation remained in force until the Carnation Revolution of 1974.

There were close links with the Catholic Church. The Concordat with the Vatican in 1940 repealed many of the anti-clerical policies of the First Republic and the Church took over religious instruction in state schools. Church building showed the new relationship. Begun in 1904, and inspired by the *Sacré Coeur* in Paris, the building of the Temple of the Sacred Crown of Jesus at Viana do Castelo had been interrupted in 1910 as the republic sought to separate Church and state. Resumed in 1926, it was finished in 1959. The commitment to Catholicism was demonstrated in the massive basilica begun in 1928 and completed in 1953, built as a focus for the large-scale pilgrimage to Fátima that had begun with a vision of the Virgin Mary being seen by three peasant children in 1917. The *Cristo Rei* statue on the heights above Almada opposite Lisbon, built in 1949–59, was on the model of that in Rio de Janeiro, which is far larger.

The Church was led by Cardinal Manuel Gonçalves Cerejeira, Patriarch of Lisbon from 1929 to 1971, a personal friend of Salazar. In contrast, António Ferreira Gomes, Bishop of Oporto, was in practice exiled for ten years from 1959 to 1969 for privately writing to Salazar in 1958 criticising government policy for in effect promoting poverty and social inequality and therefore helping communism. Salazar did not appreciate criticism.

Salazar had scant time for fascism, which he saw as anti-clerical. His dictatorship was based on tradition rather than on fascist modernity. In addition, Salazar was backed by the exiled Manuel II, and thus won the support of most monarchists. Seeking the backing of those he saw as moderates, Salazar benefited from the widespread relief that greeted stability after the disorder of 1910–26 and from the ability of Catholic corporatism to win him considerable support. Social cohesion was presented as an alternative to class division and political sectionalism.

At the same time, this was very much not a democratic system. The new legislature, the National Assembly, could only have members of the National Union (*União Nacional*), the Salazarist movement, while the parallel Corporative Chamber had official representatives, including of the official workers' syndicates that were supported in place of free trade unions, which were outlawed as were political parties. The labour legislation was based on that of fascist Italy. The President had much constitutional power, but Carmona left Salazar in control, although he became irritated with him and intrigued against him in the late 1940s.

The new constitution was approved in a national referendum in 1933, the 99.52 per cent listed as voters in favour including the large number of abstentions. The following year, the leadership of the National Syndicalists or Blue Shirts was purged as Salazar underlined his opposition to fascism, prefiguring the tension in Hungary and Romania between right-wing regimes and fascists. Salazar faced wide-ranging opposition, including a monarchist revolt in 1935, and a revolt by the crews of two warships in Lisbon in September 1936. This opposition was suppressed and those convicted (in special summary courts) sent to the new, deadly, Tarrafal prison camp in the Cape Verde Islands. There were also prisons in and near Lisbon and on São Tomé, in all of which political prisoners were held. The attempted coup led to the imposition of loyalty oaths on all civil servants. En route to Mass, Salazar, moreover, survived an assassination attempt by an anarcho-syndicalist in 1937. The following year, a bulletproof Mercedes Benz, which survives in the car museum in Caramulo, was ordered for Salazar. This was a dictatorship under the guise of a republic.

Salazar supported Francisco Franco in the Spanish Civil War (1936–9), providing the Nationalists with a key source of supplies, as well as a volunteer force, the so-called *Viriatos*, of 4000 to 5000, although the reported number varies. However, Salazar did not join Italy and Germany in their public commitment, let alone extent of support. In 1938, Portugal recognised Franco's government, which was then clearly winning the war, and in March 1939, as Franco won, signed the Iberian Pact, which was a non-aggression pact and a treaty of mutual support against any attack on either. The pact was expanded in July 1940, after the Fall of France. Given Franco's support for Hitler, this was an alignment that, while dictated by a search for security, was also scarcely that of clear neutrality. At the same time, the fate of Spain was scarcely encouraging for Portugal. For Germany, which had intervened from the outset on Franco's side in the Spanish Civil War, there were ideological and geopolitical goals, but also an economic strategy. Hitler sought a new European economic order in which Germany would become the leader of a European space free of Anglo-American influence and with the goals and terms of central planned rationalisation and specialisation set in Berlin. By early 1939, Germany was taking three-quarters of Spain's exports, so that Spain was brought into an informal *Reichsmark* sphere. The sectors targeted were iron ore, pyrites, copper, tungsten (wolfram) and foodstuffs.

The Second World War

During the Second World War (1939–45), although Japan occupied its colony of East Timor in 1942, Portugal was neutral, in line with Salazar's view of the damaging impact of the First World War on the country. Indeed, as part of the process by which the country made money by trading with both sides, Portugal sold tungsten, a basis for the strengthened steel used in particular for tanks, to both, Salazar resisting Allied pressure not to do so to Germany. Salazar did not wish to offend the then victorious Germany in the early 1940s or to provide Spain with an opportunity to attack Portugal, which Franco certainly considered. Portugal was Europe's largest source of tungsten and the industry was a major source of jobs and revenue. However, the army thwarted Salazar's attempt to please the Germans by ending the commemoration of the country's role in the First World War. Alongside Eire, Portugal flew flags at half-mast after the death of Hitler. Macao was not occupied by the Japanese but in 1943 they intimidated the Portuguese into accepting 'advisors' who, in effect, ran it. In 1945, American aircraft attacked Macao.

Neutrality ensured that Portugal became a place of refuge for those escaping the trials of war and persecution, from Jews to kings. Estoril became known as the 'Coast of Kings', and the Palace Hotel there contains a gallery of photographs of the royalty who stayed there, many during the war. The hotel was also a popular haunt of spies. German spies were able to tap the Cable and Wireless cables. Others operated out of Portuguese colonies. Some Portuguese exiles from Salazar's rule returned to Portugal to take refuge from German power only to be confined, as Bernardino Machado was on his estate on his return from France in 1940. The Portuguese Communist Party, however, although banned, encouraged illegal strikes in 1942–3.

Hollywood films of the early 1940s presented a sanitised view of Portugal and the Salazar regime, compared to their coverage of Franco's Spain. The American Office of War Information encouraged this account, which romanticised local living conditions and did not discuss the fascist practices of the Salazar regime. In October 1943, in a key development in the battle of the Atlantic, Portugal permitted Britain to establish the Lajes air base on the Azores, the Americans following with the Santa Maria base in November 1944. This provided a crucial capability in closing the mid-Atlantic 'air gap' in Allied air cover against U-boats, notably what the Germans termed the 'Black Pit' west of the Azores. In June 1944, Salazar finally yielded to Allied pressure to stop tungsten exports to Germany which, by then, was clearly going to lose the war.

The Post-War Salazar System

The provision of the Azores bases helped ensure that Portugal, much to the disappointment of those Portuguese who wanted change, was viewed far more favourably by the United States after the war than Spain, which had also been neutral. Indeed, in 1948, Portugal became a founding member of the Organisation for European Economic Co-operation, which was important in the justification and allocation of aid through the American Marshall Plan. Portugal was the sole dictatorship to receive Marshall Plan aid and obtained $70 million in 1950–1. In 1949, Portugal was a founding member of the North Atlantic Treaty Organization

(NATO). American influence led to a degree of modernisation including the bringing together in 1952 of the army and naval air services in order to create an air force. In 1957, Queen Elizabeth II paid a formal state visit. Moreover, Portugal was one of the founding members of the European Free Trade Association (EFTA) in 1960, and of the Organisation for Economic Co-operation and Development in 1961.

Domestically, the regime, which won the rigged elections of November 1945, continued to be authoritarian and reasonably united. There was opposition, but it was divided, politically, socially and over tactics. Moreover, the regime actively sought to suppress opposition. In 1948, a movement for liberalisation, the Movement of Democratic Unity, founded in October 1945, was banned. A large number of Communist activists were arrested in 1949. There was opposition to the regime within the army but, in October 1946, the Mealhada revolt did not prove the major military uprising that had been anticipated. Another rebellion by left-wing officers failed the following April.

Close links were maintained with Spain, although Franco was opposed to Portugal joining NATO without Spain. The dining room where Franco and Salazar met in 1950 can be visited in the nineteenth-century Neoclassical Brejoeira Palace near Monção.

In 1965, with Salazar's approval, the secret police assassinated Humberto Delgado, who would have won the presidential election of 1958 had it been held fairly. Delgado, an air force general, had promised if he did so to dismiss Salazar. His campaign was linked to large pro-reform demonstrations in Lisbon and Oporto. After the election, which was won by Admiral Américo Tomás, a Salazar loyalist, Delgado was expelled from the military, went into exile in Brazil and Algeria, and founded the Portuguese National Liberation Front. He mounted an unsuccessful mutiny in Beja barracks in 1962. With the support of the Spanish secret police, Delgado was lured back into Portugal near Olivenza, supposedly to meet members of the opposition, and was murdered.

Meanwhile, political prisoners continued to be held, although Álvaro Cunhal, the Communist Party leader, managed to escape from Peniche in 1960.

The 1958 election led to a constitutional change taking the choice of president away from the popular vote, with the risk of unpredictability it posed, and, instead, toward the National Assembly which was under Salazar. In 1962, riot police suppressed demonstrating students in the University of Lisbon. They were complaining at the closure of student organisations associated with opposition to the government. There was renewed pressure for change in 1968.

With its backward agriculture, Portugal continued to be poor. The production of coal, iron and oil was nugatory, although there was electricity thanks to hydro-electric power, with the first power station reliant on the dam built from 1946 at Castelo de Bode on the River Zêzere. There was a lack of investment, in large part due to the protectionist corporatist nature of the economy combined with Salazar's pronounced policy of fiscal caution. This ensured that there was no basis for domestic investment, while foreign investment and competition were constrained. In particular, the large-scale American investment and new production techniques that were so important in much of Western Europe were not really matched in Portugal.

As with Spain, the 1960s, however, saw an expansion in the tourist industry. The opening of an airport at Faro in 1965, an immediate success, combined with the spread of jet aircraft and the growing prosperity of Northern European workers to encourage sun-and-sand tourism to the Algarve.

The economy did not provide the jobs for a growing population, nor indeed prosperity for most of them. Economic development was limited. Emigration continued to Brazil, and was encouraged to Angola. In addition, there was emigration to Venezuela and, on a large-scale, to France, Germany, Switzerland, Luxembourg and Belgium. The government did not try to stop this. Others went elsewhere, for example to South Africa. Many of those who emigrated to France were political exiles. Large numbers settled in Paris where many concierges were Portuguese.

Alongside emigration, there was more limited compulsory education than elsewhere in Western Europe and higher illiteracy rates, and that despite the building of over 7000 new schools in the 1940s and 1950s. Much housing was poor and often without running water or electricity. Notwithstanding the dictatorship, however, there was some economic and social progress in the 1950s and 1960s. Indeed, it was that progress that helped turn the country against Salazar and his successor, Marcelo Caetano.

Salazar's Ideology

In the face of growing international pressure for decolonisation, pressure that kept Portugal out of the United Nations until 1955, Salazar supported an ideology of imperial development. In the Colonial Act of 1930, Salazar had centralised the administration of the overseas territories and advocated bringing the colonial population into the Portuguese nation by means of assimila-tion, although, in practice, most Africans were to continue living according to their tribal traditions. Specific hardships included the need to pay taxes in Portuguese currency, which obliged them in effect to work as forced labourers in order to get the money. To Salazar, Portugal's role and mission in large part arose from its colonies, and he also endorsed the ideas of Lusotropicalism asso-ciated with Gilberto Freyre, a Brazilian writer.

The global ideology of Salazarism, one that located Portugal's colonies in a world mission, and that led to these colonies being renamed overseas provinces in 1951, was explained in the second edition of the *Atlas de Portugal* by Aristides de Amorim Girão (1895–1960), Professor of Geography at Salazar's university, Coimbra. Published there in 1959, the atlas included as a pro-logue a section on how Portugal was 'born' and 'spread over the world' that had not been in the 1941 first edition. The preface to the second edition, published in facing columns in English and Portuguese, expounded the Portuguese theory of colonisation:

> The second edition of the *Atlas of Portugal*, whilst still addressed to the author's countrymen, has a special purpose: to make better known to foreigners a country which many people still regard as merely a Spanish province . . . There are also many fallacies concerning the geography of Portugal – alike of Portugal at home and of Portugal overseas – circulating in foreign books. For some minds are still influenced by mistaken ideas of colonialism and are unable to understand how a nation may be a complete entity although dispersed throughout the world without continuous land boundaries.

Portugal was described as a nation 'whose lot it was to fulfil an exploratory and civilising mission without equal', and cartography was seen to have a role in showing:

> the organic whole that . . . overseas provinces . . . form with the Mother Country . . . the cartographical presentation of certain little-known facts will perhaps help towards a better understanding of how these different plots of land are, finally, just so many other members of a huge national organisation with a maritime base, which, in obedience to an essentially Christian and humanitarian idea of unity, and in the geopolitical realisation of the evangelical mandate, *Euntes in mundum universum*, struck deep roots in the soil of four continents.

The section on 'How Portugal was born' consisted of nine maps mostly devoted to the war with the Muslims. The facing text ended: 'Portugal thus comes into being; and its worldwide missionary call is immediately confirmed in St Anthony of Lisbon (1190–1231) ... making his voice heard over nearly the whole of Europe as may be seen by the journeys he undertook.' Portugal's historic Christian mission was further revealed in the five maps and facing text of the section 'How Portugal spread over the World'. The fourth map presented Lisbon as the New Rome, and the fifth, which showed the journeys of the sixteenth-century Spanish Jesuit missionary St Francis Xavier, the Apostle to the Far East who 'typified ... the great missionary and civilising activity of Portugal', was entitled 'Goa, "Rome of the East"'. Xavier was mostly active in, and from, the Portuguese Empire where John III sponsored Jesuit missionary activity, helping forward the Jesuit idea of an empire of apostles. The empire was presented in the atlas as natural and organic, and not as the consequence of conquest. This was an ideology that gave Portugal apparent meaning. A 1934 map overlapped the Portuguese metropolitan and colonial territories with Europe showing how 'Portugal is not a small country'.

Under Salazar, Portugal's history, both taught and celebrated, focused on the Middle Ages and the Age of Discovery, and not on modern times, which, instead, threatened to draw attention to divisions within the country. Commemorative monuments, such as that near the cathedral at Oporto, and the restoration of buildings were designed accordingly. Thus, the twelfth-century tower of the castle at Lamego was restored as part of the celebrations for the 800th anniversary of independence in 1139. Built in 1187, the castle at Bragança was heavily restored in the 1930s; the castle of Guimarães following in the 1940s. From 1939, the government transformed the remains of the castle of Almourol, making it 'more medieval' with the addition of crenellations. The castle was made an official residence of the Portuguese Republic. In 1940, work began on repairing the castle at Monsanto, work that continued for two more years and that resumed in 1957–8.

A somewhat different legacy was the *Portugal dos Pequenitos* begun in Coimbra in 1938, and with the first phase opened in 1940. This was a park offering scaled-down replica versions of typical buildings in parts of Portugal, notably the north. The second phase consisted of monuments and heritage sites, and the third phase, finished at the end of the 1950s, provided coverage of the overseas empire as well as of Brazil. The site still has about a third of a million visitors annually.

The year 1940 was a key date for the commemoration of the past as it was that of the Portuguese World Exhibition, which was designed to mark 800 years from the foundation of the country and 300 years from the restoration of independence. Held in the *Praça do Império* in Belém, there were over three million visitors. Carmona opened the exhibition, with Salazar in attendance. Empire was a key element in an exhibition that really focused on the past. There were major exhibits from all the colonies, and Brazil, then under a dictator with his own *Estado Novo*, was the sole independent state invited. A replica of a seventeenth-century galleon was a major sight, as was a monument to Portugal's explorers, which was constructed of wood, unlike the concrete *Monument to the Discoveries* constructed at Belém in 1960 for the 500th anniversary of the death of Henry the Navigator who is the leading sculpture in the impressive, indeed inspiring, monument. Two years later, a maritime museum was opened in the west wing of the Jerónimos museum. Henry was widely celebrated, including in 1960 by tiles put up on the outside wall of a historic church in western Oporto. Another echo of the age of exploration was the armillary spheres that topped many new state buildings in the 1940s; constructed in a traditional-style, they were condemned by critics as 'soft Portuguese' on the grounds that they lacked artistic creativity.

A museum replete with the ruralist and traditionalist values of the Salazar regime was the Museum of Portuguese Folk Art opened in Lisbon in 1948. It showed local costumes and other traditional handicrafts. This was in accordance with the idealisation by the Catholic Right of the Minho region, the birthplace of Portugal.

The emphasis on things to see has been related to the stress under Salazar on a regime in which the public was expected to be more passive and docile than in Mussolini's Italy and Hitler's Germany. The mass rallies of the latter were very much not the tone of Salazar's Portugal.

Empire Under Pressure

The Museum of Design in Lisbon occupies the central site of the former bank that handled the currencies of Portugal's colonies. In the former bank's lobby, there is a colourful and large wall mosaic from 1962 depicting Portugal's colonisation of Africa from the fifteenth century. The mosaic itself is a reference back to Roman methods of decoration, including in Portugal. The colonisation is presented in benign terms, with friars teaching natives, other natives farming, and the Portuguese soldiers not shown engaged in any violent acts. Ethnic harmony, progress and Christian pros-elytisation under Portuguese leadership were the key themes. Attractive, misleading, but convenient for Portugal which, in 1962, was confronting the outbreak of revolution in Angola.

Risings in Angola (1961), Guinea-Bissau (1963) and Mozambique (1964) each and, even more, together posed a more serious and long-lasting problem. The Portuguese were able to retain control of the towns, for example crushing a rising in Luanda, the major city of Angola, in 1961. Nevertheless, they found it impossible to suppress rural opposition. In addition, their opponents could operate from neighbouring states. Guerrillas moved from attacks on border villages to a more extensive guerrilla war that sought to win popular support and to develop liberated rural areas.

Due to military commitments in Angola, the Portuguese had reduced their presence in Goa to 4000 troops and, in 1961, the

Indians overran it with 71,000 men in one day. There was little fighting. The Americans, although allied to Portugal in NATO, refused appeals for help. Diu and Damão in India were also captured. Also in 1961, Dahomey obliged Portugal to abandon São João Baptista de Ajudá, which had been an active Portuguese Atlantic trading port in the eighteenth century and a Portuguese possession from 1865. At the time of its abandonment, at only five acres and two inhabitants, it was the smallest recognised political unit in the world. Portugal did not recognise this annexation until the effective end of empire in 1975.

Eusébio, a Stunning Footballer

Moving from Mozambique to join Benfica, a leading Portuguese club, in 1961, Eusébio (1942–2014) was an accomplished striker. Of mixed race background, he made his name scoring hat-tricks in 1961, had his debut for Portugal later that year, and helped Benfica beat Real Madrid in the European Cup final the following May with two goals. He scored nine goals in the 1966 World Cup, although Portugal was beaten by England in the semi-final.

Greatly expanding the size of the army, the Portuguese fought hard in Africa, using tactical air support, helicopters, napalm and aggressive herbicides. They also sought support both from Cold War allies and from white-run governments, notably South Africa. In the early 1960s, the white-dominated Central African Federation (now Zambia, Zimbabwe and Malawi), then part of the British Empire, actively supported the white cause in Congo after the Belgian pull-out in 1960, leading to international policies at variance with those of Britain, including separate negotiations with Portugal. After Southern Rhodesia unilaterally declared independence from Britain in 1965, it also aligned with Portugal with which it had a frontier in Mozambique. Indeed, Southern Rhodesia became much more vulnerable to attack once the Portuguese eventually withdrew from Mozambique in 1975.

Earlier, the Portuguese benefited greatly from divisions among their opponents, especially between the MPLA and UNITA in Angola, and from the support of the white-rule apartheid government of South Africa. Moreover, they were able to control many key rural areas, especially the central highlands of Angola. Until 1974, the 70,000-strong Portuguese army in Angola, supported by secret police, paramilitary forces, settler vigilantes and African informers, effectively restricted guerrilla operations there and, more generally, protected the 350,000 white settlers in the colony.

By then, the revolutions had become more challenging. Opposition to Portuguese rule looked back to earlier resistance to the imposition of imperial rule, as among the Bakongo of northern Angola, but it was affected by a growing politicisation in terms of more 'modern' political ideologies, notably revolutionary socialism. There was direct reference to the Mao Zedong principles of revolutionary war, as well as training by advisers from the Soviet Union, China and Cuba, and a provision by them of more advanced weapons, although many did not arrive in any quantity until the early 1970s. Anti-personnel and anti-vehicle mines affected Portuguese mobility, while Soviet SAM-7 missiles hit their low-flying aircraft and helicopters. From 1973, the latter shifted the balance of military advantage in Guinea-Bissau, and from 1974 in Mozambique.

These missiles contributed to a sense that the Portuguese had lost the initiative. Although the Portuguese were reasonably successful in Angola, failure elsewhere sapped support for the war in the army and in Portugal. Alongside growing military dissatisfaction with the war, there was popular hostility to conscription,

with many fleeing abroad in order to escape it, part of the changing, but continual, diaspora of energy and talent under Salazar.
The war effort cost close to 40 per cent of public spending, and
the percentage of the total population involved in the war was
considerably greater than that of the Americans in Vietnam.
Portugal's gains from the global economic growth of the 1960s
were spent on an intractable war.

Caetano in Power, 1968–74

By the time of failure in Africa, Salazar was dead. In 1961, he had
survived the attempt by General Júlio Botelho Moniz, the new
minister of defence, to persuade President Américo Tomás, the
victor in 1958, to dismiss the aged Salazar. Instead, the general
was dismissed. The episode, however, was evidence of division
and discontent within the military. Each was to be more obvious
than in the case of Spain in Franco's last two decades.

In August 1968, the seventy-nine-year-old Salazar suffered a
cerebral haemorrhage when he fell from a chair while staying in
the Estoril fortress. He was replaced in September by Marcelo
Caetano, although he lingered on until 1970, being allowed,
when he recovered lucidity, to believe that he was still prime
minister, and with fake cabinet meetings held accordingly. One
of the more surprising aspects of his legacy is the Harry Potter
character Salazar Slytherin, who derives from J. K. Rowling's
immersion in Portuguese life while in Oporto. Slytherin built
the Chamber of Secrets.

Caetano was a conservative politician who long held office
under Salazar, initially as head of the Portuguese youth organisation, later as minister of the colonies, president of the Executive
Board of the National Union and minister attached to the
Presidency of the Council of Ministers, the latter effectively the
number two to Salazar. In power, Caetano was ready to help economic growth and, in what was presented as the 'political spring',

sought to lessen repression, for example easing censorship and permitting independent trade unions, which has led to later, somewhat misleading, comparisons with Mikhail Gorbachev of Russia. The opposition was allowed to run in the 1969 elections, although the government won every seat. However, some places were granted to the so-called 'Liberal Wing', a number of young technocrats whose support Caetano had won.

Caetano, however, was unwilling to maintain his reform policies. He lost the support of the 'Liberal Wing' from 1971 and, in 1973, yielded over policy to pressure from President Tomás and the regime's hardliners.

In addition, Caetano had no intention of abandoning the opposition to colonial independence movements. Isolated, the government was increasingly under strain, from both without and within, and the authoritarianism and internal cohesion that had sustained the Salazar regime were sapped by changes within society. At the same time, there was no significant international action against the Portuguese government other than in Africa. Change in Portugal would depend on the position within. So also with Spain.

Brazilian Parallels

As in Portugal after 1910, the republican coup in Brazil in 1889 led to instability. The leader of the 1889 coup, Field Marshal Deodoro da Fonseca, became head of state, while army officers benefited from salary increases, influential appointments and an increase in the size of the army. Force became normative, with Deodoro resigning in 1891 in the face of a naval revolt in support of the Vice President, Floriano Peixoto, an army leader who had played a key role in the 1889 coup. The authoritarianism of the latter led to a fresh naval revolt. It was unsuccessful in the face of army support for the government, but military rule came to an end for a while after the presidential election of 1894.

José de Almada Negreiros and Fernando Pessoa

A child of the wider Portuguese Empire, Almada Negreiros (1893–1970), the painter of Portuguese modernism, was born in São Tomé, the son of a Portuguese father and a Santomean mother. Educated in Lisbon, he introduced Portugal to Futuristic aesthetics in 1917. During the Salazar years, he acted both as an 'artistic agitator' criticising society and attacking conformism and mediocrity, and as an 'aligned' artist, producing public mural paintings. His works include a black-red portrait of Fernando Pessoa (1888–1935), which is held in the Modern Art Centre in Lisbon. Pessoa was the greatest Portuguese poet alongside Camões and the leading literary figure of twentieth-century Portugal. In 1915, he played a key role, alongside Almada Negreiros, in introducing modernism into Portugal. An active writer and literary critic, Pessoa was committed to Lisbon and there are two statues to him there. Critical of the instability of the republic, Pessoa became disenchanted with Salazar.

As with Portugal, Brazil declared war on Germany, which it did in October 1917 as a result of German submarine attacks and American pressure. However, only a small naval squadron was eventually dispatched, and it did not see active service.

Again, as with Portugal, there was instability in the 1920s. There were small-scale military revolts in 1922 and 1924, but these were suppressed by the loyal majority of the army and finally defeated in 1927 after an attempt to take refuge in the interior had failed. However, in 1930, the government was overthrown when the army proved unwilling to resist a rebel force advancing on São Paolo, the economic and political centre of the country. The rebellion, which began on 3 October, stemmed from an unwillingness to accept the verdict of the presidential election of March 1930, which had rewarded the dominant oligarchs of the state of São Paulo. Instead, claiming an overseeing right as custodians for the nation, the army seized power on 24 October before, on 3 November, handing it to Getúlio Vargas, the leader of the revolt, and the defeated candidate in March. In turn, federal forces suppressed a large-scale revolt against Vargas in São Paulo in 1932, as well as a small-scale communist rising in 1935. In 1937, Vargas used troops to dissolve Congress, declared a state of national emergency, and established the *Estado Novo*, in which he enjoyed near dictatorial powers. He remained president until 1945.

Unlike Portugal, Brazil, which did not have pro-German Spain as a neighbour, joined the Allies in the Second World War. An attempted fascist coup in 1938 had encouraged a reliance on the United States. Brazil eventually followed the United States in declaring war on Germany and Italy. It did so on 22 August 1942 in response to submarine attacks. The navy and air force helped the Allies in the Atlantic war with German submarines in 1942–5; and 25,000 troops were sent to fight as part of the Allied army in Italy in 1944–5.

Like Salazar, Vargas followed a protectionist policy. Vargas returned to power in 1950, this time democratically elected, holding power until 1954. However, concern about communism and instability led the military, eager to impose progress and order, to take over power in 1964. Very different to the Portuguese coup a decade later, this was supported by the United States. The coup produced a dictatorship that lasted until 1985 and that initially brought, alongside the killing of dissidents, economic growth in the 1970s, only to end up in the 1980s facing serious economic problems and major unpopularity.

As a result, an election in 1985 produced an opposition president and, in 1988, a democratic constitution was introduced.

Since then, Brazil has remained a democracy with an element of statist corporatism. In 2018, the Brazilian army head rejected talk of a new military dictatorship as the product of the victory in the presidential election of Jair Messias Bolsonaro, a candidate who had been an army officer and who praised the 1964–85 regime. No such outcome is likely for Portuguese politics.

12. The Carnation Revolution to the Present, 1974–

Coup and Changes

A coup on 25 April 1974 by the *Movimento das Forças Armadas* (MFA; Armed Forces Movement) was successful. This was a radical movement within the armed forces, essentially of junior army officers. There was scant resistance, and certainly less than in 1910 when the monarchy was overthrown. Only four people were killed. As in 1917, an unpopular war led to an army revolt that won power. Troops unhappy about being sent abroad were significant in both revolts. The government surrendered power to General António de Spínola, a critic of the direction of the war, whose seniority made him more acceptable than the MFA with whom Spínola sympathised. Caetano and Tomás fled to exile in Brazil.

The 1974 coup led to the release of political prisoners, the legalisation of a free press, and of the Socialist and Communist parties, and the abolition of the secret police. It is known as the Carnation Revolution because red carnations were given to the soldiers. It was followed, however, by a period of instability that lasted until 1976 and that was more disturbed and unpredictable than the immediate aftermath of the death of Franco in Spain in 1975.

After initial celebrations, the new government, the *Junta de Salvação Nacional* (National Salvation Junta), became increasingly radical, nationalising much of the economy and collectivising the land. This direction led Spínola to resign as president on 30 September after he had failed to stop the leftward move. Social tension increased, with the Communists, under Álvaro Cunhal, active in land reform and using direct action to achieve their goals, a process that enjoyed support in the more radical Alentejo. Land reform, however, proved particularly unpopular in northern and central Portugal, where much of the land was run by small family farms (unlike the estates of the south), and where a strongly entrenched and popular Catholic Church found itself the target of Communist Party agitation. The Archbishop of Braga, Francisco Maria da Silva, was an active opponent of this agitation.

In the 25 April 1975 elections for the Constituent Assembly, the first free election in Portugal since 1925, the Communists only won an eighth of the vote, mostly in the south. This reflected their lack of popularity. Instead, the Socialists dominated Lisbon, the Algarve and the centre, and the Popular Democratic Party, which drew on the liberal wing of the Marcelist party, that of Caetano, the north. The Socialists did more than three times as well as the Communists, which led to Communist talk of gaining power through a coup. It seemed possible that Portugal would become not only a left-wing, one-party state, challenging NATO, of which it was a member, from within Western Europe, but also a communist one. Henry Kissinger, the American Secretary of State, feared that Portugal would be lost to 'the enemy bloc'. He saw Portugal as potentially another Chile where a left-wing government had been overthrown in a right-wing military coup in 1973.

The increasingly conservative Spínola had fled into exile after the earlier failure of the attempted right-wing counter-revolution on 11 March 1975. However, in the context of an atomisation of the supporters of the Carnation Revolution, the Portuguese Communists lacked sufficient support within the army, and this led to the failure of an attempted coup on 25

November 1975 by elements of the army opposed to a rightward move of the government. Thanks to a mass anti-Communist mobilisation of opinion in the summer of 1975, with large-scale rallies and demonstrations, it was clear that the proposed dissolution of the Constituent Assembly by the Armed Forces Movement would face significant opposition. This prospect both empowered civilian politicians and affected opinion within the army.

Moreover, the Soviet Union did not intervene. Portugal had no contiguous border with a communist state, the Soviets had no direct overland connection to Portugal, and Soviet maritime links to it were shaky. Although recently expanded, the Soviet navy was greatly outmatched in Atlantic waters and lacked an amphibious warfare component. Portugal remained in NATO, and the army and the Socialists held the Communists off.

In February 1976, the army handed over power to civilian politicians and in that April's elections, again on the 25th, the Socialists were again the leading party and the Communists made only a modest improvement to 14.4 per cent. The Social Democratic Party achieved the second biggest vote. To create a majority coalition, the Socialists turned to the relatively right-wing Democratic and Social Centre, which came third with 16 per cent. It was the first election held after the promulgation of the new constitution approved earlier, on 2 April 1976.

This was not the end of the crisis, but it was the beginning of the end. In part thanks to serious economic strains, not least due to the transition to a post-imperial economy, the Communist vote increased to 18.8 per cent in the election on 2 December 1979, but, on the left, the Socialists at 27.3 per cent remained both the leading party and moderate. The Democratic Alliance, a coalition of the Social Democratic Party, the Democratic and Social Centre Party and two small parties, won 45.2 per cent of the popular vote and a majority of the seats. The Agrarian Reform Law of September 1977 provided a generally acceptable limit to

collectivisation, essentially restricting it to the big estates in the south, notably the Communist stronghold in the Alentejo. About 1,200,000 hectares, 31 per cent of the south, had been occupied in 1975–6. The government had scant alternative to the legalisation of the process.

In turn, the democratic system was sufficiently grounded to enable the replacement of the Socialist government by a right-of-centre one of the Democratic Alliance in January 1980. Under Francisco Sá Carneiro, this government had a populist flavour but also pushed through privatisation measures. The collectivi-sation in the Algarve was largely reversed. In the election held on 5 October 1980, the Communist percentage of the vote fell to 16.8, the Socialists won 27.8 and the Democratic Alliance coa-lition rose to 47.6. Sá Carneiro, who had founded the Popular Democratic Party in 1974, renaming it the Social Democratic Party in 1976, remained prime minister.

Meanwhile, in 1975, Portugal withdrew from its colonies, both East Timor and the colonies in Africa including the Cape Verde Islands where the independence process had been peace-ful. Three-quarters of a million people from the large settler populations returned to Portugal with few possessions and with a potent sense of grievance. Many remained for years in hastily erected housing in shantytowns on the edge of Portuguese cities, especially Lisbon, and this brought a degree of edginess to both politics and society.

With time, however, the tension was eroded, in large part due to the benefits of economic growth that became particularly apparent after Portugal joined the EEC in 1986. Portugal had applied to join in 1977 as a key aspect of a political normalisa-tion and international acceptance that had already been seen when it was admitted to the Council of Europe the previous year. It was not to join, however, until 1986 because its entry was linked to that of Spain. The latter admission faced several problems, not least strong French concerns about agricultural competition. However, the process of joining and, therefore, of wishing to be seen as acceptable was important in encouraging moderation and modernisation in Portuguese politics. There was no equivalent to the attempted, but unsuccessful, Spanish coup of 1981 with its tanks on the streets and takeover of the *cortes*.

The legacy of the *Estado Novo* was not, subsequently, a key element in political dispute. In part, this was because there was, in effect, a pact of forgetting between the political parties, but also because there was no political movement of weight looking back to the Salazar dictatorship. There was no past on offer that was attractive, not least because Portugal's imperial position, which had been significant to the ideology of the *Estado Novo*, was totally gone. The Salazarist system did not have as strong a political afterglow as monarchy had had in the 1910s and 1920s. Moreover, unlike in Spain, the military was not the basis for political action from the right.

The post-dictatorial governments did see a degree of restitution, notably for the reputation of Humberto Delgado, Salazar's opponent who was assassinated in 1965. Mário Soares, the Socialist prime minister from 1976 to 1978 and 1983 to 1985, had supported Delgado, and had his remains interred in the National Pantheon. Delgado was also retrospectively promoted to field marshal, and Lisbon airport was named after him in 2015. Much that was named by, or after, Salazar was renamed. Thus, the *Ponte Salazar* over the Tagus at Lisbon, a suspension bridge modelled on the Golden Gate Bridge, was renamed the *Ponte 25 de Abril*. There are numerous *Praças 25 de Abril* and the date became a national holiday known as Freedom Day. A very different public art was pushed to the fore, with statues of trade union activists, as in Régua, and of workers. Thus, in Alcochete on the southern shore of the Tagus estuary, a centre of saltpans, a statue of a salt worker was erected in 1985 with the inscription 'From Salt to Rebellion and Hope'.

The 1980s

Sá Carneiro died in December 1980 in a plane crash that is widely attributed to assassination. He was succeeded by Francisco Pinto Balsemão, but the latter faced a divided party and also a general strike. In the election held on 25 April 1983, the government did badly and, instead, Soares won with 36 per cent of the vote. However, as this was very much a minority, the result led to a coalition with the Social Democrats (who had won 27.2 per cent) in what was called the Central Block.

The pressures involved in preparing to join the EEC led to economic strains, as did a more general policy of economic modernisation and fiscal austerity. There was opposition from both right and left, with the *Forças Populares de 25 Abril* (FP-25), opposed to the amendments to the constitution, seeking a communist revolution, and staging terrorism from the left from 1980 to 1987. Eighteen people were killed by the FP-25 which, aside from bank raids to fund itself, attacked the American embassy in 1984 and NATO ships in Lisbon in 1985.

Soares resigned in June 1985 due to a lack of parliamentary support, and fresh elections were held on 6 October 1985. They were won by Aníbal Cavaco Silva, the new leader of the Social Democratic Party, with 29.9 per cent of the vote and eighty-eight seats. The Socialists only won 20.8 per cent. Soares, however, became president in 1986, serving, after re-election in 1991, until 1996.

Once in the EEC, from 1986, Portugal benefited from economic access to the European market, from investment that brought new technology as well as funds, and from financial aid. Cavaco Silva, the Social Democratic prime minister from 1985 to 1995, pushed ahead with deregulation, tax cuts and modernisation, including with labour law reforms that led to the laying off of workers who had to be compensated, which increased government debt. There was much new building of roads and bridges with EEC funds. In Lisbon, the massive, prominent and unappealing, Amoreiras shopping centre opened in 1985. Old buildings were swept aside for office blocks, and cobbled streets were tarmacked. The revisions of 1982 and 1989 removed the revolutionary and socialist provisions in the constitution. The former extinguished the Council of Revolution created in 1975, and reduced presidential powers, thus speeding the 'civilianisation' of the regime and strengthening parliamentary control over it. The latter revision allowed for privatisation.

The 1990s

Growth stalled with the widespread recession of the early 1990s, and, in 1992, the year of its presidency of the European Union, Portugal only remained in the exchange rate mechanism (ERM) of the EEC with difficulty. Moreover, Portugal's backward agriculture found it hard to compete, not least with the more mechanised production of French and Spanish agriculture. Economic access to the European market meant European access to the Portuguese market, and to a degree that had not been fully explained to the public. This competition was enhanced by the consequences of the Single European Market, which was introduced in 1986. Combined with strikes and corruption, the government was undermined, and Cavaco Silva, who had won impressive majorities in the 1987 (50.2 per cent of the popular vote) and 1991 (50.6 per cent) elections, decided not to contest the 1995 election.

The election of that year, held on 1 October, was won by António Guterres, the Socialist leader, with a major swing from the Social Democrats, and the Socialist candidate also won the presidential election in 1996. Guterres continued the fiscal straitjacket that enabled Portugal to join the European Economic and Monetary Union, the basis of the euro, in 1999. In 1998, Lisbon was the site of the Expo World Fair, for which the Vasco da Gama

Bridge across the Tagus was built. Moreover, the Portuguese novelist José Saramago won the Noble Prize for Literature in the same year. An atheist and communist, his work, notably the critical *O Evangelho Segundo Jesus Cristo* (*The Gospel According to Jesus Christ*, 1991), had offended the Cavaco Silva government.

Guterres was re-elected on 10 October 1999, the Socialists missing an absolute majority by only one MP. They won 44.1 per cent of the vote and 115 seats (compared to 43.8 per cent and 112 the previous time), while the Social Democratic Party won 32.3 per cent and 81, the People's Party (on the right) 8.3 per cent and 15, and the Communists 9 per cent and 17. The Socialists were foremost in most districts, but not in the north-east where the Social Democrats led.

The 2000s

Economic and fiscal problems in the early 2000s led Portugal to breach the 3 per cent deficit ceiling in 2000, while unemployment rose, as did emigration, including to Angola and Mozambique. Corruption scandals accentuated the sense of crisis. The collapse in 2001 of a Douro road bridge with many casualties caused a scandal as the government had ignored advice that it needed repair. A monument survives at the site. There was also a systemic failure to provide adequate quality housing for the rapidly expanding population in Lisbon. The Socialists did badly in local elections in December 2001, and Guterres resigned that month. He went on to be elected Secretary-General of the United Nations in 2016.

The elections in March 2002 brought the right-of-centre Social Democratic Party under José Manuel Barroso to power. As prime minister, Barroso focused on trying to cut the public deficit, although with only limited success. He stood down (becoming president of the European Commission until 2014), to be replaced in July 2004 by Pedro Santana Lopes, the Mayor of Lisbon. Lacking the mandate of winning office by an election, Santana Lopes was widely regarded as incompetent.

The government was defeated in the election of 20 February 2005, which was won by the Socialists. They took 121 seats on 45 per cent of the vote, up from 96 the previous time (2002), and won in 19 of the 22 electoral districts, including in districts that historically voted against them. The centre-right parties lost over 11 per cent of the vote they had won then, while the Left Bloc did well, winning 6.4 per cent of the vote. José Sócrates, the Socialist leader, was to be prime minister until 2011, winning re-election in 2009. He had to push through fiscal austerity and structural reforms. This included an unpopular cutting of facilities in rural areas, notably elementary schools and medical facilities.

In the 2009 election, held on 27 September, the Socialists won the largest number of seats, but lost 24 seats and 9 per cent of the votes, so that they no longer had a majority of the 230 seats in the Portuguese Assembly. The Social Democrats increased their share by six seats, the Left Bloc by eight and the People's Party by nine. As the left overall won a majority of the votes and seats, Sócrates was invited to form the new government. The Socialists had done particularly well in the south, centre and north-west, the Social Democrats in the north-east, the People's Party in the north, and the Left Bloc in the Algarve and the upper Tagus Valley.

The 2010s

Already affected by the EU's need to fund new member states from Eastern Europe, and with a large debt ratio, Portugal was in a very poor position to confront the global financial crisis that began in 2008. The economy shrank, while pressure from the EU, the IMF and the European Central Bank to cut the prominent public debt led, in 2010, to brutal new austerity measures that contributed to unemployment, which, for those under twenty-five, rose to over 40 per cent by 2013, greatly encouraging emigration. The government found itself in a very difficult position. Parliament rejected an austerity package on 23 March 2011 and, in response, Sócrates, whose Socialists were in a minority, resigned, leading to the 2011 snap election.

In office in the meanwhile as head of a caretaker government, Sócrates had to seek a bailout in order to avoid the bankruptcy threatened by concern about the public finances and about a lack of competitiveness in the economy. These failures encouraged moves in bond prices linked to the worries of bond traders and rating agencies. This bailout came in the shape of €78 billion from the IMF, the Eurozone and the European Central Bank, a bailout, agreed on 16 May 2011, that lasted until May 2014. In return, the government had to accept cutting its budget deficit from 9.8 per cent of GDP in 2010 to 3 per cent in 2013. In July 2011, Moody's, the leading rating agency, had cut the country's credit rating to junk status. Portugal went through many of the problems that Greece faced as a result of the global crisis.

The crisis was not the best basis for the elections held on 5 June 2011. The Social Democrats, under Pedro Passos Coelho, did unexpectedly well, winning 108 seats (81 in 2009), compared to 74 for the Socialists (97), 8 for the Left Bloc (16), 24 for the People's Party (21) and 16 for the Communists (15). The Social Democrats won seventeen out of the twenty districts in the country, including Lisbon, Oporto, the Algarve and the Azores. The Socialist percentage of the vote fell from 36.6 to 28, while that of the Social Democrats rose from 29.1 to 38.7. Socrates resigned as general secretary of the party that night. The Social Democrats formed a government with the support of the People's Party.

There was not the violence that was to be seen in Greece. Benefit cuts led to large demonstrations in 2012, albeit peaceful ones. Pensioners were hit particularly hard, but so also were most families. Coelho, the Social Democratic prime minister from 2011 to 2015, pushed through the changes required by the bailout. Privatisations and higher taxes were part of the equation. A political crisis was surmounted in July 2013.

The 2015 election, held on 4 October, saw a vote against austerity and a fall in support for the right-wing coalition of the Social Democratic Party and the People's Party, the two parties losing 12 per cent from the support they had won in 2011. They won Lisbon, Oporto and the north, but the south voted for the Socialists. Coelho failed to form a sustainable minority government, and António Costa, the Socialist leader, became prime minister. His parliamentary majority included the Left Bloc, the Communists and the Greens. In accordance with his electoral promises, many of the austerity policies of the previous government were reversed, with state pensions, wages and working hours restored to the levels of the 2000s. Economic growth was accompanied by a fall of the budget deficit to 2.1 per cent of GDP in 2016. In the 2017 local elections, the Socialists did well. However, the public debt remained high and there was a lack of the necessary structural reforms in the economy.

In the late 2000s and 2010s, the dissension over the economic-social crisis led some historians on the right to praise Salazar and the stability he had brought, a parallel to the revision on behalf of Franco and Mussolini already seen in Spain and Italy. In contrast, on the left, there was criticism of the failure of Portugal to modernise during his regime, criticism that led to counterfactual speculation about what would have happened otherwise. The breakdown in a united view on the past was an aspect of the strength of partisan politics in a period of acute economic difficulties and also of the foundation of a broader-based right.

Social Issues

Alongside political change, there has been social transformation since the Salazar years. This transformation is clearly marked with legislation and in popular attitudes. The first has brought the legalisation of divorce (2001, into effect 2002), abortion (2007), homosexual civil relationships (2010) and, in 2017, adoption by homosexuals.

Abortion became legal as a result of a referendum. The first, conducted on 28 June 1998, was the first national referendum in post-Salazarist Portuguese history and was proposed by the Communist Party. A law legalising abortion had gone through the Assembly, but the leaders of the Socialist and Social Democratic parties had agreed on a referendum; 50.91 per cent voted against, with the north showing a majority against, and Lisbon and the south a majority for. The variations by district were very great, from 81.9 per cent yes in Setúbal to 82.8 per cent no in the

---

Decriminalising Drugs

In 2001, the Socialist government changed the drug law. Illegal drugs remained illegal and dealers were still to be prosecuted, but possession for personal use ceased to be a criminal offence. Instead, those caught are instructed to visit the Commission for Dissuasion of Drug Addiction. Opiate substitutes are available to all users who wish to quit and there is an engagement with therapy. In the 1990s, amid public concern and a sense of social crisis, about 1 per cent of the population were heroin users, a high rate of HIV infection was a related problem, and drug-related crime was serious. The openness and prosperity that followed the Salazar regime was partly responsible. At present there are about 33,000 heroin users and in 2016 there were 27 fatal overdoses. The number of newly diagnosed HIV cases among drug users has fallen, as have hepatitis infection rates. Drug-related crime also appears to have fallen, while the price of most illicit drugs fell.

Azores. A second referendum was held on 11 February 2007, in accordance with an election pledge by the Socialists. The Social Democrats were divided, as they had not been in 1998. This time 59.25 per cent of those who voted, voted yes. The more conservative north (but not Oporto) voted no, but the cities, the south and most of the centre voted yes.

Popular attitudes have seen radical changes in behaviour. The percentage of marriages ending in divorce is high: about 62 per cent within three years. Moreover, about 52 per cent of babies are born to parents who are not married. Attendance at church has fallen, and notably so among the young. If people still go to church for weddings and christenings, and show a commitment to local saints and the linked festivities, that scarcely matches earlier patterns of observance.

The continued role and ambition of Catholicism can be seen with the enormous new basilica at Fátima that was inaugurated in 2007, the new cathedral inaugurated in Bragança in 1996 and, more modestly, with the annual pilgrimages to the Chapel of Our Lady of Lapa near Sernancelhe, a site that has attracted pilgrims since the start of the sixteenth century. In 2009, Pope Benedict canonised Nuno Álvares Pereira, the victor at Aljubarrota in 1385, who had later become a mystic. However, the reality of religious commitment, in a country where 97 per cent of the population remains at least nominally Catholic, was very different to much of this clerical action.

None of this is unique to Portugal. Indeed, similar changes can be found in such Catholic centres as Ireland, Italy and Spain. They are part of a crisis of European Catholicism. Yet, that did not make the change less significant for Portugal. It was also linked, as in other Catholic countries, to a marked drop in the birth rate. Many couples no longer married, but, whether married or not, couples began having children later, and had fewer. This fed through into a major and apparently permanent change in the population structure. The size of the population was increasingly due to the growing percentage of pensioners and not to those of the young and fertile. In European terms, Portugal indeed has a population among those that take the least exercise. Concern grew about a likely fall in the population, indeed a substantial one that would make it harder to support the growing percentage of elderly dependents. Portugal, today, has one of the oldest populations in Europe. Back in the 1960s, the ratio of active to inactive in the population was 1:2. Today it is closer to 1:5, which makes the sustainability of the welfare state a hot topic politically.

Again, Portugal was not unique. The remedies discussed included that of trying to persuade emigrants and their descendants to return to Portugal. This remedy, however, suffered from both push and pull elements. There was some reverse migration during the growth years of the late 1990s but it then stopped. Of the states where many Portuguese had emigrated, France, Britain, Switzerland, Luxembourg and the United States continued to offer good prospects. Thus, both the National Health Service and Boots advertised in Portugal for employees and, when last seeing a pharmacist in the Boots branch in Exeter, I found that the two on duty were both Portuguese. Once emigrants settled in Britain and elsewhere, they met partners and tended to settle down. In London, part of Stockwell became a little Portugal with about 27,000 Portuguese and a number of restaurants, although the Portuguese were distributed more widely across London, including in Notting Hill and Brent. The 2011 census revealed 95,065 Portuguese-born residents in the United Kingdom (41,041 in London), and in 2013 the Office of National Statistics estimated a figure of 107,000. The community really developed in the late 1990s as unemployment rose in Portugal. In 2001, the census figure was 36,555. Some estimates are far higher than 100,000. Outside London, Norfolk was the county with the largest number.

Good prospects were less consistently the case in Brazil, while the significant Portuguese community in Venezuela fled from there in the late 2010s, some back to Portugal. However, there was no equivalent to the return of Portuguese from the colonies that had occurred in the mid-1970s. Portugal's economy did not offer good prospects, and notably so for the young. The prospects were best in the Lisbon area and in Oporto, and their urban image replaced that of a rural country; but those were the very areas that least needed immigration. Greater Lisbon has a population of over two million. Indeed, the rise in rent there in 2018, a rise that greatly exceeded inflation, led to demonstrations in both cities against Airbnb, which was accused of removing properties from the rental market to the benefit of tourists. Tourism focused on both cities. Across the country as a whole in 2017 there was a 17 per cent increase in tourism revenue.

The pressure on rent underlined the extent to which different interests competed. Regenerated city-centre slum property was

---

Euro 2016

Portuguese national pride swelled on 10 July 2016 with televisions on across the country as Portugal beat France in the 109th minute in the *Stade de France* in Paris. I was in Lisbon that night, and the atmosphere was certainly electric. The Madeira-born captain, Cristiano Ronaldo, has repeatedly won awards and is a champion goal-scorer. Portugal had organised Euro 2004, only to lose the final against Greece. In Euro 2016, Portugal's first major tournament triumph, Ronaldo was the second-highest goal-scorer, but was stretchered off the pitch in the final. The man of the match, Brazilian-born Pepe, had moved to Portugal in 2001 and made his name playing for Porto in 2004–7. The year after winning Euro 2016, Portugal won the Eurovision Song Contest for the first time.

---

acquired by the wealthy while ordinary workers moved to the urban edges. There were calls in 2018 from the Communist Party for an increase in the state pension, which indeed is very low. This puts pressure on family economies when the (fewer) young cannot support their parents who now, on average, live longer than in previous generations.

The small towns of the interior increasingly appear deserted by the young, their roadside cafés filled, instead, by old men sipping their memories, while wives and widows go to church to mumble prayers for distant grandchildren. This situation is most acute in areas where the farming could not compete with European competitors. Portugal suffered not only from the opening up to competition that followed entry into the European Union, but also from the consequent accession to the latter of the food-exporting states of Eastern Europe. Spanish agriculture has fared much better. Looking to the future, European attempts to help the economies of north-west Africa will further accentuate the competitive problem. Population moves from the land again were not new, nor unique to Portugal, but they contributed greatly to a sense of malaise.

13. The North

The bustling waterfront of Oporto is a world away from the hilltop village of Castelo Rodrigo. Yet, there is a common element in the north, that of an identity that is very much not that of Lisbon. Aside from a longstanding rivalry between Oporto and Lisbon, there is a feeling in the north that its concerns are not valued in the capital. The beers certainly compete. Super Bock tends to be drunk in the north and Sagres in the south. The most visible rivalry stems from football, with Porto against Sporting Lisbon and Benfica.

Within the north, the principal difference is between the oceanic west and the inland east. The former has an Atlantic climate. It is damp and often cloudy. Cloud, mist and drizzle restrict sunlight and thus lessen the growing season. Coming off the sea, the prevailing westerly winds are also salt-laden. Steep slopes lead to a high run-off of water, ensuring that valley bottoms are often affected by rivers and streams in spate. Over the centuries, heavy rainfall has helped wash soil from the uplands. This ensures that they have poor, frequently acidic, soils which lessen their suitability for continuous or intensive cultivation, especially in the absence of fertilisers. Poor soils, however, can also be found in lowland areas, many of which have been affected by erosion.

The rain brings much tree growth. It also helps account for a café life in Oporto that is frequently indoors, as well as for rural buildings with thick walls designed to keep out the rain. Many are built of granite.

In contrast, the north-east is arid. In the rain-shadow cast by the mountains of the north-west, Trás-os-Montes (Beyond the Mountains) in the north-east is also very hot in the summer, often

---

Port

A key example of the continuing cooperation of Britain and Portugal, port wine reflects the longstanding practice of vine cultivation in the Douro Valley, probably from the Roman period on. Wine from the area became important to Britain as an alternative to that from France, but posed a problem because it was bitter and did not travel well. As a consequence, it is believed that British merchants in the seventeenth century first added brandy in order to make the wine stronger, sweeter and, therefore, a product that travelled well to Britain. The combination of the method with British purchasing power produced a successful wine industry and one that spread its sales around the British Empire.

The legacy in northern Portugal is still impressive, from the vineyards of the Douro region to the port lodges in Oporto in which port is matured and bottled. Both are a must for tourists to the region. There are several types of port: ruby, tawny and white. Each has a particular character, and then there are the specific vintage and late-bottled vintage ports.

---

over 40 °C, and cold in the winter. Across much of it, although not in the remote Montesinho national park, there are relatively few trees, and, instead, an often sparse cover of vegetation. The grazing is generally not good. Oswald Crawfurd, British Consul in Oporto from 1867 to 1891, noted in his *Travels in Portugal* (1875): 'a country of upland rye-fields, vines, chestnuts, and cork-trees, but showing much bare, reddish-yellow soil – a district neither fertile nor picturesque'.

The weather and the soil are not the sole problems, as much of the north is mountainous, with heights of up to 6500 feet. This encourages a pattern of the intensive cultivation of small plots, a process seen for example in wine-growing and one that was encouraged by the historical division of holdings among sons. These difficulties ensured that the region had a disproportionate share of the emigration of the late twentieth century. Indeed, in the 1960s to 1990s, the region lost nearly a third of its population. Abandoned buildings are a common sight.

The remoteness of the region encouraged the development of distinctive dialects, notably Portuguese-Spanish Rionorês in the border village of Rio de Onor, and a distinctive language, Mirandês, in and near the frontier town of Miranda. Officially recognised as a second language in 1998, this is close to the language spoken under Roman rule. The region also has pagan-style traditions, notably fertility ritual-like customs, as well as the *pauliteiros* (stock dancers) of the Miranda region who are like English Morris dancers.

The history of the region is one of the origins of Portugal, but also of power moving southwards, first to Coimbra and then to Lisbon. The traditional power centres, Braga, Guimarães and Oporto, are the cities where history is most present. Each is impressive, and contains striking medieval buildings. The centre of Guimarães became an UNESCO World Heritage site in 2001 and the city was European Capital of Culture in 2012.

Power takes a number of historical forms. The most prominent are cathedrals, castles and palaces. At the same time, Oporto, European City of Culture in 2001, also presents a very different form of power, that of commerce and youth. Whereas many of the small towns are very quiet in the evenings, that is not the case in Oporto.

Visiting the north, the focus for travellers tends to be on alcohol, notably the massed barrels of maturing port that can be seen in the Gaia area on the south bank of the Douro opposite the centre of Lisbon. Port is drunk in many ways. I have been served it hot with sugar, apples and cinnamon, in a riverside bar in the vineyard region. Given the switchback nature of many of the roads, it is best if the non-drinkers drive. Not well-known outside Portugal, the reds of the region are also very impressive. The light *vinho verde* (green wine) of the coastal lowlands of the Minho are even more delightful when drunk there. The wine should be drunk green, in other words very young, and sometimes has a greenish tint.

There are also distinctive dishes, including tripe in Oporto; the locals are known as *tripeiros*. It tastes less awful than elsewhere because served/disguised in a spicy mix including beans and sausages. Meat-filled open-sandwiches, called *Francesinhas*, are another of the city's distinctive dishes. Good, fresh fish is readily found along the coast, notably sardines. Grilled eels are a winter speciality in the Minho.

Tourism focuses on Oporto and on the Douro Valley where, once river levels were controlled by dams, tourist cruises began in 1986, and where the Alto Douro wine region has been a

---

Partying on the Douro

In 1733, the British in Oporto celebrated the feast of St George:

> both sexes gathered, dressed in costly gala dress, at a *quinta* on the banks of the Douro, in view of a large number of vessels and adorned with flags, streamers and pennants, which fired repeated volleys of artillery. There were masquerades, trips on the river in little boats with music, dancing and a magnificent meal, to which the consuls of other nations were invited, and this entertainment lasted until seven o'clock the next day.

UNESCO World Heritage site since 2001. Many more boats have recently been commissioned, and tourists can cruise in comfort. The granite city, Oporto, has benefited from entry into the European Union and from becoming a UNESCO World Heritage site. Its spacious airport is a good point of entry and is reached by the Metro.

14. The Centre

The Beiras, Estremadura, Ribatejo and the environs of Lisbon ensure that central Portugal is highly diverse, both physically and in its human geography. Portugal's most fertile areas are found here, as well as key historical sites. The winter is relatively mild, except in Beira Alta and especially in the snowy Serra de Estrela. Drought is not a serious problem. As a result, agriculture is easier than to north or south. However, on the plateau of Beira Alta to the east, the dryness reduces the options for farming.

The 'centre' includes areas that are not well-known to tourists, such as Beira Alta and the sparsely populated Beira Baixa, but also what Oswald Crawfurd in the early 1870s termed: 'the "show places" of Portugal – Coimbra, with its university – Tomar, with its fine conventual church – Alcobaça, with the remains of its magnificent Cistercian monastery and its abbey . . . Batalha, with its inimitable architecture . . . Mafra, with its huge eighteenth-century palace and convent – and Sintra, with its shaded groves and Moorish castle.' All remain musts, with the addition of Óbidos. Mafra's library is most impressive but, like Klosterneuburg near Vienna and the Escorial near Madrid, its closest equivalents due to the palace-monastery character conspicuously not seen at Versailles, Mafra is not a site that matches most modern interests. Sites in the central regions range from ancient remains to the fortress at Peniche where the cells of Salazar's most important political prison can be visited.

The Beiras capture anew the variety of Portugal, in this case from the sandy beaches of Beira Litoral and the historic charm of the university city of Coimbra, to the craggy heights of the Beira Alta, and the arid, partly empty, Beira Baixa. Further south, Estremadura and Ribatejo are more fertile and busier, with attractive, ocean-sprayed, coastal beaches matched to the east by the energy and lushness of the Tagus Valley.

Lisbon stands on its own, a world city whose far-flung empire has gone, but that has discovered a new vitality in recent years and become much more attractive to tourists. The largest number of international tourists go to Lisbon. In 2016, the majority of tourists there were Europeans, with the British, Spaniards, French, Germans, Dutch and Italians being most significant. *Time Out* and other international news publications have been referring to Lisbon as the 'Best European Tourist Destination', and deservedly so. Lisbon is also important as a centre of the Portuguese-speaking world, although it competes in that with São Paulo and Rio de Janeiro, each of which have larger populations.

Historically, the Phoenicians were followed in Lisbon by the Greeks, Carthaginians and Romans. The archaeological museum holds interesting finds, while a ruined theatre can be seen in the Museum of the Roman Theatre and, in a busy part of the city, the calm Gothic cloister by the cathedral includes the remains of a Roman street. The *Núcleo Arqueológico* contains the remains of a Roman fish-preserving factory.

The Suevi were followed by the Visigoths, both of whom left little in Lisbon or, indeed, central Portugal. Conquered by the Moors in 714, what was called *Al-Ushbuna* was held by them until 1147. Captured after a bitter siege, Lisbon became the capital in 1255, replacing Coimbra, which was not a port and which was now deemed too far north.

The wealth brought by transoceanic expansion from the fifteenth century on left a legacy in magnificent buildings, especially the marvellous Jerónimos monastery in Belém. Much of the city and many prominent buildings were destroyed in the 1755 earthquake. However, thanks to Pombal's commanding energy, Lisbon was then rapidly rebuilt. This is most clearly seen in the *Praça do Comércio* and the grid of Baixa to the north.

'The Finest Women in the World'

John Swinton, chaplain to a British warship, recorded in Lisbon in 1730:

> Today I saw a young Portuguese lady exceeding beautiful with fine pendants in her ears richly attired with very delicate features and an exceeding fine complexion, though I suspect she might be painted, for the Portuguese ladies paint almost from their infancy and it is reckoned no crime amongst them, though some give not into this abominable custom, but preserve their natural fine complexion, and of these I have seen several since I came to Lisbon, who are certainly, whether we consider their exceeding graceful fine shape, their delicate features, their charming air and address, their vivacity and poignancy of wit or lastly their attractive winning behaviour, the finest women in the world. The ladies of quality and gentlewomen of fashion seldom go out except to church.

Lisbon's wealth and significance were shadowed in the early nineteenth century when the royal court moved to Brazil (1807) and then when Brazil became independent (1822). Subsequent political instability in the nineteenth century, while damaging, was less significant than the extent to which the city and country were bypassed by greater growth elsewhere in the Atlantic world, and notably so in the commercial and wider influence of Britain. The wealth of Atlantic commerce focused on Liverpool, London and Glasgow.

In the twentieth century, the same process continued, with coups in 1910 and 1926, bookending a period of acute instability.

Under Salazar, Lisbon did not have the bombastic building seen in Mussolini's Rome, and, compared to Franco's Madrid, did not bear the marks of war. However, alongside some important buildings that remain to the present, there was a degree of stagnation.

A relative lack of growth after the Second World War left the city looking seedy, and the coup of 1974 did not greatly change this. For example, the *Praça do Comércio* was in effect a parking site in the 1980s.

Redevelopment, in contrast, largely followed membership of the European Community in 1986. Inward investment was linked to economic growth that owed something to lower taxes and to the general global economic expansion of the mid-late 1980s. The expansion of the Metro, the first station of which was opened in December 1959, was an important symbol of modernity. Lisbon became a tourist destination that produced more money for investment as well as a more attractive restaurant world.

Lisbon now certainly does not have the buzz of Barcelona, but the city is extremely varied, from the stately to the interestingly rundown in the Alfama. It is also rapidly changing. For the new part of Lisbon, the visitor should go to the *Parque das Nações*, the site of the 1998 World Exhibition.

Moreover, the wider area, including, in particular, Belém, Cascais and Sintra, offers much in addition to see. All three can be easily reached from Lisbon by public transport and are musts. Sintra's riches include the royal palace, the ruined Moorish castle and the Capuchin monastery. The pastries in the *Fábrica das Verdadeiras* can be strongly recommended and make the walk from the railway station more pleasant. Belém is fascinating, but has crowds, notably in and around Jerónimos monastery. These crowds are less pressing in the more modest pleasures of Cascais where, away from the ugly modern marina, it is worth finding the calmness of the Guimarães museum and the relaxation of the nearby municipal park.

More generally, Lisbon and the region bring together the twin strengths of fish and pork. There is plenty of fresh fish on display, as well as shellfish. Suckling pig is a speciality, especially in Coimbra. Stews are common, as is the one-time staple of dried salted cod. Desserts are not particularly distinguished. Food is better value than in other Western European capitals and portions are generous. This is not a wine region of note, but Ribatejo wines from the nearby Tagus Valley have much improved recently, there are wines from Estremadura to the north, including whites from Bucelas, and wine from around Portugal can readily be drunk in the capital. Lisbon is also a beer town, with *cervejarias* or beer halls that are sometimes extensively tiled. There are plentiful cafés and some very attractive *pastelarias* (cake shops). I can recommend eating outdoors at the *Académica* in the Largo do Carmo and, for fish, in outdoor restaurants near the military museum.

15. The South

The south (the Alentejo and the Algarve) is dominated by plateaux, and the coastal plains are small. The winter is not harsh and there is a long growing season, but the summer drought poses a major problem. Grain, cork, sheep, olives and pigs are key elements of the agriculture of this region, and the fields are large. Visiting in the early 1870s, Oswald Crawfurd wrote: 'The maize and wheat fields of the north and centre of Portugal are replaced in Algarve . . . by orchards of figs and of almond trees.'

The Chapel of Bones or ossuary in Évora, a seventeenth-century work in which the poorly lit walls and pillars are decorated with the skeletons of about 5000 monks, is one of the most vivid sights in southern Portugal. There is another in Faro. My first tour of Portugal included a visit to Évora and I still recall the ossuary, the heat of the streets and the flatness of nearby lands after the rolling topography further north.

To most British tourists, southern Portugal is the Algarve, and notably its south coast. Particularly from 1974, its almond orchards and sleepy villages were transformed into hotel resorts. The year 2017 was a record year tourism in Portugal, with 20.6 million visitors and 57.5 million overnight stays, but, in 2018, there was a decline in tourism to the country, and notably in the Algarve. Nevertheless, its combination of beaches, sun and golf helped sustain tourism, a process encouraged by difficulties in Egypt, Greece, Morocco, Tunisia and Turkey, all rival markets.

The diversity of the Algarve coast is significant, but, against the backdrop of the products of a variety of geologies, there is a series of splendid beaches, and east of Faro the water is generally warm and calm while the beaches are sandy. The nearby towns are not always as attractive. Alongside a mass of villas, there are hotels, apartment blocks, and an infrastructure of bars, clubs and restaurants that varies in its appeal. Aside from tourists, there are many British expatriates living in the Algarve. Some towns, such as Faro, are far more attractive than others, for example Praia da Rocha. The west coast, with its colder and rougher sea, the most dramatic section of the country's 516-mile-long coastline, is less developed than the south coast, while inland Algarve offers a set of rural attractions and historic small towns that tend to be overlooked in favour of the coast, for example Silves and its interesting medieval castle.

The Algarve had the series of settlers and traders seen elsewhere. Celts by land, and Phoenicians (with settlements at Tavira and Castro Marim) and Carthaginians (settlements included Lagos) by sea, were followed by Romans who used irrigation to increase agricultural production. The major Roman site is at Milreu near Faro where there are the ruins of a large villa from the first century CE. Aside from the remains of the baths, there are mosaics depicting fish. The municipal museum of Faro, the Roman port Ossonoba, includes the third century CE 'Mosaic of the Ocean'. A Roman coast road from Spain to Faro included a seven-arched bridge at Tavira.

The Romans were followed by the Suevi and Visigoths. Relatively few buildings survive from that period. There was, however, a continuance of the Christianisation seen in the later Roman period. Thus, at Milreu, the temple dedicated to the cult of water was converted into a church. In Faro, a Roman temple became the site of the cathedral.

Under the Moors, there was much settlement and a process of naming seen in particular in location names that include *Al. Al-Gharb al-Andalus*, western Andalusia, became the Algarve. Churches were converted into mosques, as at Faro and Milreu. The honeyed sweetmeats of the south, notably *figos cheios* (figs with an almond surround in the form of a flower) reflect the Moorish legacy.

Moorish rule was followed by the *Reconquista*, which was a drawn-out process. The last major Islamic town to be recaptured was Faro, by Afonso III, in 1249, although Castile challenged the claim to sovereignty over the Algarve. Tavira had been reconquered seven years earlier and Silves in 1244.

Reconquest was for Christianity, but not for Portugal, which was a recently established state. This reconquest saw the destruction and/or conversion of Islamic sites. Mosques became churches, often, as at Faro, a return to their earlier function. Castles were built both during the conquest and in order to secure it, notably from Islamic raids, but also, in the east, from Castilian attack, as at Alcoutim and Castro Marim. The latter, the headquarters of the Order of Christ from 1319 to 1334, contains the church where its lay governor, Henry the Navigator, prayed. He is celebrated also with a statue in Lagos. Henry went on to build a fortified town on the coast at Sagres in 1416, although very little remains at the world's-end site, near Cape St Vincent, that dates from his lifetime. The Algarve's ports, such as Lagos, benefited from the development of shipbuilding and trade as Portugal became a maritime and then an oceanic power.

Prior to the recent rise in tourism, the Algarve focused on fishing and agriculture. The former can still be seen in ports such as Portimão. It contains Renaissance and Baroque buildings, such as the Renaissance *Igreja da Misericórdia* in Tavira and the Baroque *Igreja de Nossa Senhora do Carmo* in Faro; but not in the number found in central Portugal. Earthquakes, notably the very destructive one in 1755, ensured that there is much building from that period, especially in Faro, where the cathedral was rebuilt and heavily gilded.

Further north, the plains of the Alentejo had a similar sequence of settlement and control, although without coastal tourism. Neolithic sites near Évora, Castelo de Vide and Monsaraz were followed in sequence by the Romans, Visigoths and Moors. A major Roman site can be visited via the remains in museums in, and near, Marvão. The *Reconquista* left far more historic buildings, notably castles, walls and churches. Thus, in Estremoz, the tower-keep of a hilltop castle-palace, built in the thirteenth century, survives. Much of the rest of the castle was destroyed in 1698 when the ammunition stored there exploded. Other surviving castles include that at Castelo de Vide.

Buildings and their sites record the sequence of control, as with the castle at Elvas, a Moorish work built on a Roman site, only to be rebuilt after recapture in 1229. At Mértola, the castle, built after reconquest in 1238, was constructed on Moorish foundations which rested on Roman remains. The mosque there was reconsecrated as a church.

The region, however, failed to develop. Instead, like much of southern Italy, what had been a prosperous agricultural region under the Romans became agriculturally backward. That has continued to the present. The small towns are full of the elderly, while the young, in this sparsely populated and often hot region, are elsewhere. This relative lack of development and the calmness of the region, however, leaves much to see for tourists interested in Portugal's past. This helps explain the survival of much wildlife, as in the *Serra de São Mamede*, a natural park near Portalegre, that contains eagles, deer, wild boar and genets, alongside the silent megaliths that mark man's passage, and possibly with greater permanence than much we build today.

There is also across the region excellent food, notably pork. As with elsewhere in Portugal, this comes in a variety of forms, including *carne de porco à alentejana*, a mixture of pork and clams. There is also lamb, as in *ensopado de Borrego*, goat, as in *cabrito assado*, and rabbit. Flavours are sealed in by means of cooking in a *cataplana*. Cooking in wine is distinctive, as is the use of coriander. The particular cheese from Serpa is the product of goat and sheep milk. The Alentejo, especially around Vidigueira, where the nearby Roman site at St Cucufate includes wine presses, and around Reguengos de Monsaraz, also produces much wine that is for drinking, not cooking, and both red and white.

16. The Islands

The Azores and Madeira, Portuguese from the fifteenth century, are problematic in economic terms. Volcanic terrain, notably in Madeira and on Faial and Pico in the Azores, is difficult to cultivate. Tourism competes with the nearer regions of the Mediterranean. Islands that were crucial as way-stations in the Portuguese maritime empire, and as ports of call or coaling stations on maritime routes to South Africa and South America, are now bereft of strategic significance.

The islands have a population that is largely of Portuguese origin, a consequence of the earlier need for peasants. This helps explain the limited nature of pressure for decentralisation, which has more support in the Azores than in Madeira, although both benefited from a special statute of autonomy in the 1976 constitution. The islands are also different. For example, the Azores benefits from plentiful rainfall, while Madeira relies on irrigation.

The Azores are far-flung, indeed over 400 miles apart. Flores and Corvo, the islands furthest into the Atlantic, feel remote. The main group of islands are Faial, Pico, São Jorge, Terceira and Graciosa. To the east are Santa Maria and the largest island, São Miguel, the green island, which has a cobbled capital, Ponta Delgada, where cruise ships stop, not least due to a recent expansion in berthing facilities. The capital's historic buildings can be complemented by the attractive and easily accessible botanical garden, which reflects historic links to Brazil and Africa, and is in better order than the also-impressive botanical garden in Lisbon. The island contains a number of volcanic craters, most notably that of Sete Cidades, a pleasant trip from the capital, as are those at Furnas where there is also an impressive garden.

The local sites include volcanic ground on the Lagoa das Furnas where food is slow-cooked underground. I can confirm that it is very tasty.

Henry the Navigator organised the settlement of the Azores. In 1671, Captain John Narbrough wrote of São Miguel: 'above the cliffs is all planted fields of corn . . . the island looks very green and is divided into fields'. His general theme for the Azores was that of plenty: 'wheat and beef and pork and other provisions . . . all provision for the life of man is plentiful'.

Of the central islands in the Azores, Terceira has the most to see. Its main town, Angra do Heroísmo, became a UNESCO World Heritage site in 1983. There was much building there during the sixteenth and seventeenth centuries, and the island is also noted for its volcanic landscape. The liberalisation of airspace over the islands of São Miguel and Terceira in March 2015 led to low-cost flights and to an increase in air passengers of 19.9 per cent in 2016 and 18.5 per cent in 2017.

Madeira is the principal island in an archipelago nearly 400 miles off the African coast. Henry the Navigator was responsible for the introduction of wheat, vines and sugar cane to the island. In 1669, Captain John Wood commented: 'The fruit of this island is sweet and sour oranges, lemons, dates, figs, walnuts, chestnuts, pomegranates, plantains, bananas, onions, but the chief is the grapes . . . fishing and a little cotton.' However, he noted of the island of Porto Santo to the north-east that it was exposed to Moroccan privateers from Sallee (Rabat). Madeira's economy is now dominated by tourists, 1.5 million in 2016, and popular with those who seek a restful sunny break. The capital, Funchal, has an attractive historic core that benefits, like other Portuguese cities, from not being fought over during the last 150 years.

To end deep into the Atlantic may seem an afterthought that is a long way from the streets of Lisbon and Oporto. Not so, for the link is a close one. Go to the island of Faial in the Azores.

You can find several other tourists, as I did, in the main town, Horta, to share a taxi to the still active volcanic landscape to the west where a volcano – the Capelinhos – erupted in 1957–8, speeding emigration from the island to the Azores. Then return and you will find the activity of Portuguese life and customs, the busyness of people on the street. There is the link through the inhabitants, very much Portuguese and living in many respects like those they are related to on the mainland. There is also the flow of a country that looks to the sea, that focuses on ports and that ends in islands.

Selected Further Reading

Alexander, Boyd (ed.), *Journal of William Beckford in Portugal and Spain, 1787–1788* (Stroud, 2005).

Anderson, James, *A History of Portugal* (Westport, CT, 2003).

Barman, Roderick, *Citizen Emperor: Pedro II and the Making of Brazil, 1825–91* (Stanford, CA, 1999).

Bennison, A. K., *The Almoravid and Almohad Empires* (Edinburgh, 2016).

Bethencourt, Francisco, *The Inquisition: A Global History, 1478–1834* (Cambridge, 2009).

Bethencourt, Francisco and Adrian Pearce, *Racism and Ethnic Relations in the Portuguese-Speaking World* (Oxford, 2012).

Bethencourt, Francisco and Diogo Ramada Curto (eds), *Portuguese Oceanic Expansion, 1400–1800* (Cambridge, 2007).

Birmingham, David, *A Concise History of Portugal* (2nd edn, Cambridge, 2003).

Chakravarti, Ananya, *The Empire of Apostles: Religion, Accommodation and the Imagination of Empire in Early Modern Brazil and India* (India, 2018).

Clarence-Smith, Gervase, *The Third Portuguese Empire, 1825–1975: A Study in Economic Imperialism* (Manchester, 1985).

Diffie, Bailey Wallace and George Winius, *Foundations of the Portuguese Empire* (Minneapolis, 1977).

Disney, A. R., *A History of Portugal and the Portuguese Empire* (New York, 2009).

Eliade, Mircea, *The Portugal Journey* (New York, 2010).

Fisher, Stephen, *The Portugal Trade* (London, 1971).

Francis, A. D., *The Methuens and Portugal* (Cambridge, 1966).

—, *Portugal, 1715–1808: Joanne, Pombaline and Rococo Portugal as seen by British Diplomats and Traders* (London, 1985).

Hatton, Barry, *The Portuguese: A Modern History* (Northampton, MA, 2011).

—, *Queen of the Sea: A History of Lisbon* (London, 2018).

Jack, Malcolm, *Lisbon, City of the Sea: a History* (London, 2007).

—, *Sintra: A Glorious Eden* (London, 2002).

Kaplan, Marion, *The Portuguese: The Land and Its People* (Manchester, 2006).

Levenson, Jay (ed.), *The Age of the Baroque in Portugal* (New Haven, CT, 1993).

Linehan, Peter, *Historical Memory and Clerical Activity in Medieval Spain and Portugal* (London, 2012).

Livermore, Harold, *A New History of Portugal* (Cambridge, 1966).

—, *The Origins of Spain and Portugal* (London, 1971).

—, *Portugal: A Traveller's History* (Woodbridge, 2004).

—, *The Twilight of the Goths* (Bristol, 2006).

Livermore, Harold and W. J. Entwistle (eds), *Portugal and Brazil* (Oxford, 1952).

Lochery, Neill, *Out of the Shadows: Portugal from the Revolution to the Present Day* (London, 2017).

Macaulay, Neill, *Dom Pedro: The Struggle for Liberty in Brazil and Portugal, 1798–1834* (Durham, NC, 1986).

Marques, António Henrique de Oliveira, *Daily Life in Portugal in the Late Middle Ages* (Madison, WI, 1971).

—, *A History of Portugal* (New York, 1979).

Kenneth Maxwell, *The Making of Portuguese Democracy* (Cambridge, 1995).

—, *Pombal: Paradox of the Enlightenment* (Cambridge, 1995).

Mayson, Richard, *Port and the Douro* (London, 2004).

Meneses, Filipe Ribeiro de, *Portugal 1914–1926: From the First World War to Military Dictatorship* (Bristol, 2004).

—, *Salazar: A Political Biography* (New York, 2009).

Meneses, Filipe Fibeiro de and R. McNamara, *The White Redoubt, the Great Powers and the Struggle for Southern Africa, 1960–1980* (London, 2017).

Newitt, Malyn, *Emigration and the Sea: An Alternative History of Portugal and the Portuguese* (London, 2015).

—, *A History of Portuguese Overseas Expansion* (London, 2004).

—, *Portugal in European and World History* (London, 2009).

Newitt, Malyn and Martin Robson (eds), *Lord Beresford and the British Intervention in Portugal 1807–1820* (Lisbon, 2004).

Opello, Walter, *Portugal: From Monarchy to Pluralist Republic World* ((Boulder, CO, 2017).

Paquette, Gabriel, *Imperial Portugal in the Age of Atlantic Revolutions: The Luso-Brazilian World, c. 1770–1850* (Cambridge, 2013).

Payne, Stanley, *A History of Spain and Portugal* (Madison, WI, 1973).

Pinto, António Costa (ed.), *Contemporary Portugal: Politics, Society and Culture* (New York, 2003).

—, *Salazar's Dictatorship and European Fascism* (New York, 1996).

Raby, D. L., *Fascism and Resistance in Portugal, 1941–1974* (Manchester, 1988).

Ramos Pinto, Pedro, *Lisbon Rising: Urban Social Movements in the Portuguese Revolution, 1974–75* (Manchester, 2013).

Robinson, Richard, *Contemporary Portugal* (London, 1979).

Russell, Peter, *Prince Henry 'the Navigator': A Life* (New Haven, CT, 1960).

Russell-Wood, A. J. R., *The Portuguese Empire, 1415–1808: A World on the Move* (Baltimore, MD, 1998).

Saraiva, José Hermano, *Portugal: A Companion History* (Manchester, 1997).

Saramago, José, *Journey to Portugal: In Pursuit of Portugal's History and Culture* (San Diego, CA, 2000).

Sardica, José Miguel, *Twentieth-Century Portugal: A Historical Overview* (Lisbon, 2008).

Subrahmanyam, Sanjay, *The Career and Legend of Vasco da Gama* (Cambridge, 1997).

Trindale, Luís, *The Making of Modern Portugal* (Newcastle, 2013).
—, *Narratives in Motion: Journalism and Modernist Events in 1920s Portugal* (New York, 2016).
Wheeler, Douglas and Walter Opello, *Historical Dictionary of Portugal* (Plymouth, 2010).

Index